Memoirs of Casanova Volume III

Memoirs of Casanova Volume III

Giacomo Casanova

MINT EDITIONS

Memoirs of Casanova Volume III was first published in 1902.

This edition published by Mint Editions 2021.

ISBN 9781513281858 | E-ISBN 9781513286877

Published by Mint Editions®

**MINT
EDITIONS**

minteditionbooks.com

Publishing Director: Jennifer Newens
Design & Production: Rachel Lopez Metzger
Project Manager: Micaela Clark
Translated By: Arthur Machen
Typesetting: Westchester Publishing Services

Contents

I

I Renounce the Clerical Profession, and Enter the Military Service—Therese Leaves for Naples, and I Go to Venice—I Am Appointed Ensign in the Army of My Native Country—I Embark for Corfu, and Land at Orsera to Take a Walk

I had been careful, on my arrival in Bologna, to take up my quarters at a small inn, so as not to attract any notice, and as soon as I had dispatched my letters to Therese and the French officer, I thought of purchasing some linen, as it was at least doubtful whether I should ever get my trunk. I deemed it expedient to order some clothes likewise. I was thus ruminating, when it suddenly struck me that I was not likely now to succeed in the Church, but feeling great uncertainty as to the profession I ought to adopt, I took a fancy to transform myself into an officer, as it was evident that I had not to account to anyone for my actions. It was a very natural fancy at my age, for I had just passed through two armies in which I had seen no respect paid to any garb but to the military uniform, and I did not see why I should not cause myself to be respected likewise. Besides, I was thinking of returning to Venice, and felt great delight at the idea of shewing myself there in the garb of honour, for I had been rather ill-treated in that of religion.

I enquired for a good tailor: death was brought to me, for the tailor sent to me was named Morte. I explained to him how I wanted my uniform made, I chose the cloth, he took my measure, and the next day I was transformed into a follower of Mars. I procured a long sword, and with my fine cane in hand, with a well-brushed hat ornamented with a black cockade, and wearing a long false pigtail, I sallied forth and walked all over the city.

I bethought myself that the importance of my new calling required a better and more showy lodging than the one I had secured on my arrival, and I moved to the best inn. I like even now to recollect the pleasing impression I felt when I was able to admire myself full length in a large mirror. I was highly pleased with my own person! I thought myself made by nature to wear and to honour the military costume, which I had adopted through the most fortunate impulse. Certain that nobody knew me, I enjoyed by anticipation all the conjectures which people would indulge in respecting me, when I made my first appearance in the most fashionable cafe of the town.

My uniform was white, the vest blue, a gold and silver shoulder-knot, and a sword-knot of the same material. Very well pleased with my grand appearance, I went to the coffee-room, and, taking some chocolate, began to read the newspapers, quite at my ease, and delighted to see that everybody was puzzled. A bold individual, in the hope of getting me into conversation, came to me and addressed me; I answered him with a monosyllable, and I observed that everyone was at a loss what to make of me. When I had sufficiently enjoyed public admiration in the coffee-room, I promenaded in the busiest thoroughfares of the city, and returned to the inn, where I had dinner by myself.

I had just concluded my repast when my landlord presented himself with the travellers' book, in which he wanted to register my name.

"Casanova."

"Your profession, if you please, sir?"

"Officer."

"In which service?"

"None."

"Your native place?"

"Venice."

"Where do you come from?"

"That is no business of yours."

This answer, which I thought was in keeping with my external appearance, had the desired effect: the landlord bowed himself out, and I felt highly pleased with myself, for I knew that I should enjoy perfect freedom in Bologna, and I was certain that mine host had visited me at the instance of some curious person eager to know who I was.

The next day I called on M. Orsi, the banker, to cash my bill of exchange, and took another for six hundred sequins on Venice, and one hundred sequins in gold after which I again exhibited myself in the public places. Two days afterwards, whilst I was taking my coffee after dinner, the banker Orsi was announced. I desired him to be shewn in, and he made his appearance accompanied my Monsignor Cornaro, whom I feigned not to know. M. Orsi remarked that he had called to offer me his services for my letters of exchange, and introduced the prelate. I rose and expressed my gratification at making his acquaintance. "But we have met before," he replied, "at Venice and Rome." Assuming an air of blank surprise, I told him he must certainly be mistaken. The prelate, thinking he could guess the reason of my reserve, did not insist, and apologized. I offered him a cup of coffee, which he accepted, and, on leaving me, he begged the honour of my company to breakfast the next day.

I made up my mind to persist in my denials, and called upon the prelate, who gave me a polite welcome. He was then apostolic prothonotary in Bologna. Breakfast was served, and as we were sipping our chocolate, he told me that I had most likely some good reasons to warrant my reserve, but that I was wrong not to trust him, the more so that the affair in question did me great honour. "I do not know," said I, "what affair you are alluding to." He then handed me a newspaper, telling me to read a paragraph which he pointed out. My astonishment may be imagined when I read the following correspondence from Pesaro: "M. de Casanova, an officer in the service of the queen, has deserted after having killed his captain in a duel; the circumstances of the duel are not known; all that has been ascertained is that M. de Casanova has taken the road to Rimini, riding the horse belonging to the captain, who was killed on the spot."

In spite of my surprise, and of the difficulty I had in keeping my gravity at the reading of the paragraph, in which so much untruth was blended with so little that was real, I managed to keep a serious countenance, and I told the prelate that the Casanova spoken of in the newspaper must be another man.

"That may be, but you are certainly the Casanova I knew a month ago at Cardinal Acquaviva's, and two years ago at the house of my sister, Madame Lovedan, in Venice. Besides the Ancona banker speaks of you as an ecclesiastic in his letter of advice to M. Orsi:"

"Very well, monsignor; your excellency compels me to agree to my being the same Casanova, but I entreat you not to ask me any more questions as I am bound in honour to observe the strictest reserve."

"That is enough for me, and I am satisfied. Let us talk of something else."

I was amused at the false reports which were being circulated about me, and, I became from that moment a thorough sceptic on the subject of historical truth. I enjoyed, however, very great pleasure in thinking that my reserve had fed the belief of my being the Casanova mentioned in the newspaper. I felt certain that the prelate would write the whole affair to Venice, where it would do me great honour, at least until the truth should be known, and in that case my reserve would be justified, besides, I should then most likely be far away. I made up my mind to go to Venice as soon as I heard from Therese, as I thought that I could wait for her there more comfortably than in Bologna, and in my native place there was nothing to hinder me from marrying her openly. In the mean time the fable from Pesaro amused me a good deal, and I expected every day to see it denied in some newspaper. The real officer Casanova must have laughed at the accusation brought against him of having run away with the horse, as much as I laughed at the caprice which had metamorphosed me into an officer in Bologna, just as if I had done it for the very purpose of giving to the affair every appearance of truth.

On the fourth day of my stay in Bologna, I received by express a long letter from Therese. She informed me that, on the day after my escape from Rimini, Baron Vais had presented to her the Duke de Castropignano, who, having heard her sing, had offered her one thousand ounces a year, and all travelling expenses paid, if she would accept an engagement as prima-donna at the San Carlo Theatre, at Naples, where she would have to go immediately after her Rimini engagement. She had requested and obtained a week to come to a decision. She enclosed two documents, the first was the written memorandum of the duke's proposals, which she sent in order that I should peruse it, as she did not wish to sign it without my consent; the second was a formal engagement, written by herself, to remain all her life devoted to me and at my service. She added in her letter that, if I wished to accompany her to Naples, she would meet me anywhere I might appoint, but that, if I had any objection to return to that city, she would immediately refuse the brilliant offer, for her only happiness was to please me in all things.

For the first time in my life I found myself in need of thoughtful consideration before I could make up my mind. Therese's letter had entirely upset all my ideas, and, feeling that I could not answer it a once, I told the messenger to call the next day.

Two motives of equal weight kept the balance wavering; self-love and love for Therese. I felt that I ought not to require Therese to give up such prospects of fortune; but I could not take upon myself either to let her go to Naples without me, or to accompany her there. On one side, I shuddered at the idea that my love might ruin Therese's prospects; on the other side, the idea of the blow inflicted on my self-love, on my pride, if I went to Naples with her, sickened me.

How could I make up my mind to reappear in that city, in the guise of a cowardly fellow living at the expense of his mistress or his wife? What would my cousin Antonio, Don Polo and his dear son, Don Lelio Caraffa, and all the patricians who knew me, have said? The thought of Lucrezia and of her husband sent a cold shiver through me. I considered that, in spite of my love for Therese, I should become very miserable if everyone despised me. Linked to her destiny as a lover or as a husband, I would be a degraded, humbled, and mean sycophant. Then came the thought, Is this to be the end of all my hopes? The die was cast, my head had conquered my heart. I fancied that I had hit upon an excellent expedient, which at all events made me gain time, and I resolved to act upon it. I wrote to Therese, advising her to accept the engagement for Naples, where she might expect me to join her in the month of July, or after my return from Constantinople. I cautioned her to engage an honest-looking waiting-woman, so as to appear respectably in the world, and, to lead such a life as would permit me to make her my wife, on my return, without being ashamed of myself. I foresaw that her success would be insured by her beauty even more than by her talent, and, with my nature, I knew that I could never assume the character of an easy-going lover or of a compliant husband.

Had I received Therese's letter one week sooner, it is certain that she would not have gone to Naples, for my love would then have proved stronger than my reason; but in matters of love, as well as in all others, Time is a great teacher.

I told Therese to direct her answer to Bologna, and, three days after, I received from her a letter loving, and at the same time sad, in which she informed me that she had signed the engagement. She had secured the services of a woman whom she could present as her mother; she would reach Naples towards the middle of May, and she would wait for me there till she heard from me that I no longer wanted her.

Four days after the receipt of that letter, the last but one that Therese wrote me, I left Bologna for Venice. Before my departure I had received an answer form the French officer, advising me that my passport had reached Pesaro, and that he was ready to forward it to me with my trunk, if I would pay M. Marcello Birna, the proveditore of the Spanish army, whose address he enclosed, the sum of fifty doubloons for the horse which I had run away with, or which had run away with me. I repaired at once to the house of the proveditore, well pleased to settle that affair, and I received my trunk and my passport a few hours before leaving Bologna. But as my paying for the horse was known all over the town, Monsignor Cornaro was confirmed in his belief that I had killed my captain in a duel.

To go to Venice, it was necessary to submit to a quarantine, which had been adhered to only because the two governments had fallen out. The Venetians wanted the Pope to be the first in giving free passage through his frontiers, and the Pope insisted that the Venetians should take the initiative. The result of this trifling pique between the two governments was great hindrance to commerce, but very often that which bears only upon the private interest of the people is lightly treated by the rulers. I did not wish to be quarantined, and determined on evading it. It was rather a delicate undertaking, for in Venice the sanitary laws are very strict, but in those days I delighted in doing, if not everything that was forbidden, at least everything which offered real difficulties.

I knew that between the state of Mantua and that of Venice the passage was free, and I knew likewise that there was no restriction in the communication between Mantua and Modena; if I could therefore penetrate into the state of Mantua by stating that I was coming from Modena, my success would be certain, because I could then cross the Po and go straight to Venice. I got a carrier to drive me to Revero, a city situated on the river Po, and belonging to the state of Mantua.

The driver told me that, if he took the crossroads, he could go to Revero, and say that we came from Mantua, and that the only difficulty would be in the absence of the sanitary certificate which is delivered in Mantua, and which was certain to be asked for in Revero. I suggested that the best way to manage would be for him to say that he had lost it, and a little money removed every objection on his part.

When we reached the gates of Revero, I represented myself as a Spanish officer going to Venice to meet the Duke of Modena (whom I knew to be there) on business of the greatest importance. The sanitary certificate was not even demanded, military honours were duly paid to me, and I was most civilly treated. A certificate was immediately delivered to me, setting forth that I was travelling from Revero, and with it I crossed the Po, without any difficulty, at Ostiglia, from which place I proceeded to Legnago. There I left my carrier as much pleased with my generosity as with the good luck which had attended our journey, and, taking post-horses, I reached Venice in the evening. I remarked that it was the and of April, 1744, the anniversary of my birth, which, ten times during my life, has been marked by some important event.

The very next morning I went to the exchange in order to procure a passage to Constantinople, but I could not find any passenger ship sailing before two or three months, and I engaged a berth in a Venetian ship called, Our Lady of the Rosary, Commander Zane, which was to sail for Corfu in the course of the month.

Having thus prepared myself to obey my destiny, which, according to my superstitious feelings, called me imperiously to Constantinople, I went to St: Mark's Square in order to see and to be seen, enjoying by anticipation the surprise of my acquaintances at not finding me any longer an abbe. I must not forget to state that at Revero I had decorated my hat with a red cockade.

I thought that my first visit was, by right, due to the Abbe Grimani. The moment he saw me he raised a perfect shriek of astonishment, for he thought I was still with Cardinal Acquaviva, on the road to a political career, and he saw standing before him a son of Mars. He had just left the dinner-table as I entered, and he had company. I observed amongst the guests an officer wearing the Spanish uniform, but I was not put out of countenance. I told the Abbe Grimani that I was only passing through Venice, and that I had felt it a duty and a pleasure to pay my respects to him.

"I did not expect to see you in such a costume."

"I have resolved to throw off the garb which could not procure me a fortune likely to satisfy my ambition."

"Where are you going?"

"To Constantinople; and I hope to find a quick passage to Corfu, as I have dispatches from Cardinal Acquaviva."

"Where do you come from now?"

"From the Spanish army, which I left ten days ago."

These words were hardly spoken, when I heard the voice of a young nobleman exclaiming;

"That is not true."

"The profession to which I belong," I said to him with great animation, "does not permit me to let anyone give me the lie."

And upon that, bowing all round, I went away, without taking any notice of those who were calling me back.

I wore an uniform; it seemed to me that I was right in showing that sensitive and haughty pride which forms one of the characteristics of military men. I was no longer a priest: I could not bear being given the lie, especially when it had been given to me in so public a manner.

I called upon Madame Manzoni, whom I was longing to see. She was very happy to see me, and did not fail to remind me of her prediction. I told her my history, which amused her much; but she said that if I went to Constantinople I should most likely never see her again.

After my visit to Madame Manzoni I went to the house of Madame Orio, where I found worthy M. Rosa, Nanette, and Marton. They were all greatly surprised, indeed petrified at seeing me. The two lovely sisters looked more beautiful than ever, but I did not think it necessary to tell them the history of my nine months absence, for it would not have edified the aunt or pleased the nieces. I satisfied myself with telling them as much as I thought fit, and amused them for three hours. Seeing that the good old lady was carried away by her enthusiasm, I told her that I should be very happy to pass under her roof the four or five weeks of my stay in Venice, if she could give me a room and supper, but on condition that I should not prove a burden to her or to her charming nieces.

"I should be only too happy," she answered, "to have you so long, but I have no room to offer you."

"Yes, you have one, my dear," exclaimed M. Rosa, "and I undertake to put it to rights within two hours."

It was the room adjoining the chamber of the two sisters. Nanette said immediately that she would come downstairs with her sister, but Madame Orio answered that it was unnecessary, as they could lock themselves in their room.

"There would be no need for them to do that, madam," I said, with a serious and modest air; "and if I am likely to occasion the slightest disturbance, I can remain at the inn."

"There will be no disturbance whatever; but forgive my nieces, they are young prudes, and have a very high opinion of themselves."

Everything being satisfactorily arranged, I forced upon Madame Orio a payment of fifteen sequins in advance, assuring her that I was rich, and that I had made a very good bargain, as I should spend a great deal more if I kept my room at the inn. I added that I would send my luggage, and take up my quarters in her house on the following day. During the whole of the conversation, I could see the eyes of my two dear little wives sparkling with pleasure, and they reconquered all their influence over my heart in spite of my love for Therese, whose image was, all the same, brilliant in my soul: this was a passing infidelity, but not inconstancy.

On the following day I called at the war office, but, to avoid every chance of unpleasantness, I took care to remove my cockade. I found in the office Major Pelodoro, who could not control his joy when he saw me in a military uniform, and hugged me with delight. As soon as I had explained to him that I wanted to go to Constantinople, and that, although in uniform, I was free, he advised me earnestly to seek the favour of going to Turkey with the bailo, who intended to leave within two months, and even to try to obtain service in the Venetian army.

His advice suited me exactly, and the secretary of war, who had known me the year before, happening to see me, summoned me to him. He told me that he had received letters from Bologna which had informed him of a certain adventure entirely to my honour, adding that he knew that I would not acknowledge it. He then asked me if I had received my discharge before leaving the Spanish army.

"I could not receive my discharge, as I was never in the service."

"And how did you manage to come to Venice without performing quarantine?"

"Persons coming from Mantua are not subject to it."

"True; but I advise you to enter the Venetian service like Major Pelodoro."

As I was leaving the ducal palace, I met the Abbe Grimani who told me that the abrupt manner in which I had left his house had displeased everybody.

"Even the Spanish officer?"

"No, for he remarked that, if you had truly been with the army, you could not act differently, and he has himself assured me that you were there, and to prove what he asserted he made me read an article in the newspaper, in which it is stated that you killed your captain in a duel. Of course it is only a fable?"

"How do you know that it is not a fact?"

"Is it true, then?"

"I do not say so, but it may be true, quite as true as my having been with the Spanish army ten days ago."

"But that is impossible, unless you have broken through the quarantine."

"I have broken nothing. I have openly crossed the Po at Revero, and here I am. I am sorry not to be able to present myself at your excellency's palace, but I cannot do so until I have received the most complete satisfaction from the person who has given me the lie. I could put up with an insult when I wore the livery of humility, but I cannot bear one now that I wear the garb of honour."

"You are wrong to take it in such a high tone. The person who attacked your veracity is M. Valmarana, the proveditore of the sanitary department, and he contends that, as nobody can pass through the cordon, it would be impossible for you to be here. Satisfaction, indeed! Have you forgotten who you are?"

"No, I know who I am; and I know likewise that, if I was taken for a coward before leaving Venice, now that I have returned no one shall insult me without repenting it."

"Come and dine with me."

"No, because the Spanish officer would know it."

"He would even see you, for he dines with me every day."

"Very well, then I will go, and I will let him be the judge of my quarrel with M. Valmarana."

I dined that day with Major Pelodoro and several other officers, who agreed in advising me to enter the service of the Republic, and I resolved to do so. "I am acquainted," said the major, "with a young lieutenant whose health is not sufficiently strong to allow him to go to the East, and who would be glad to sell his commission, for which he wants one hundred sequins. But it would be necessary to obtain the consent of the secretary of war." "Mention the matter to him," I replied, "the one hundred sequins are ready." The major undertook the commission.

In the evening I went to Madame Orio, and I found myself very comfortably lodged. After supper, the aunt told her nieces to shew me, to my room, and, as may well be supposed, we spent a most delightful night. After that they took the agreeable duty by turns, and in order to avoid any surprise in case the aunt should take it into her head to pay them a visit, we skilfully displaced a part of the partition, which allowed them to come in and out of my room without opening the door. But the good lady believed us three living specimens of virtue, and never thought of putting us to the test.

Two or three days afterwards, M. Grimani contrived an interview between me and M. Valmarana, who told me that, if he had been aware that the sanitary line could be eluded, he would never have impugned my veracity, and thanked me for the information I had given him. The affair was thus agreeably arranged, and until my departure I honoured M. Grimani's excellent dinner with my presence every day.

Towards the end of the month I entered the service of the Republic in the capacity of ensign in the Bala regiment, then at Corfu; the young man who had left the regiment through the magical virtue of my one hundred sequins was lieutenant, but the secretary of war objected to my having that rank for reasons to which I had to submit, if I wished to enter the army; but he promised me that, at the end of the year, I would be promoted to the grade of lieutenant, and he granted me a furlough to go to Constantinople. I accepted, for I was determined to serve in the army.

M. Pierre Vendramin, an illustrious senator, obtained me the favour of a passage to Constantinople with the Chevalier Venier, who was proceeding to that city in the quality of bailo, but as he would arrive in Corfu a month after me, the chevalier very kindly promised to take me as he called at Corfu.

A few days before my departure, I received a letter from Therese, who informed me that the Duke de Castropignano escorted her everywhere. "The duke is old," she wrote, "but even if he were young, you would have no cause for uneasiness on my account. Should you ever want any money, draw upon me from any place where you may happen to be, and be quite certain that your letters of exchange will be paid, even if I had to sell everything I possess to honour your signature."

There was to be another passenger on board the ship of the line on which I had engaged my passage, namely, a noble Venetian, who was going to Zante in the quality of counsellor, with a numerous and brilliant retinue. The captain of the ship told me that, if I was obliged to take my meals alone, I was not likely to fare very well, and he advised me to obtain an introduction to the nobleman, who would not fail to invite me to share his table. His name was Antonio Dolfin, and he had been nicknamed Bucentoro, in consequence of his air of grandeur and the elegance of his toilet. Fortunately I did not require to beg an introduction, for M. Grimani offered, of his own accord, to present me to the magnificent councillor, who received me in the kindest manner, and invited me at once to take my meals at his table. He expressed a desire that I should make the acquaintance of his wife, who was to accompany him in the journey. I called upon her the next day, and I found a lady perfect in manners, but already of a certain age and completely deaf. I had therefore but little pleasure to expect from her conversation. She had a very charming young daughter whom she left in a convent. She became celebrated afterwards, and she is still alive, I believe, the widow of Procurator Iron, whose family is extinct.

I have seldom seen a finer-looking man, or a man of more imposing appearance than M. Dolfin. He was eminently distinguished for his wit and politeness. He was eloquent, always cheerful when he lost at cards, the favourite of ladies, whom he endeavoured to please in everything, always courageous, and of an equal temper, whether in good or in adverse fortune.

He had ventured on travelling without permission, and had entered a foreign service, which had brought him into disgrace with the government, for a noble son of Venice cannot be guilty of a greater crime. For this offence he had been imprisoned in the Leads—a favour which destiny kept also in reserve for me.

Highly gifted, generous, but not wealthy, M. Dolfin had been compelled to solicit from the Grand Council a lucrative governorship, and had been appointed to Zante; but he started with such a splendid suite that he was not likely to save much out of his salary. Such a man as I have just portrayed could not make a fortune in Venice, because an aristocratic government can not obtain a state of lasting, steady peace at home unless equality is maintained amongst the nobility, and equality, either moral or physical, cannot be appreciated in any other way than by appearances. The result is that the man who does not want to lay himself open to persecution, and who happens to be superior or inferior to the others, must endeavour to conceal it by all possible means. If he is ambitious, he must feign great contempt for dignities; if he seeks employment, he must not appear to want any; if his features are handsome, he must be careless of his physical appearance; he must dress badly, wear nothing in good taste, ridicule every foreign importation, make his bow without grace, be careless in his manner; care nothing for the fine arts, conceal his good breeding, have no foreign cook, wear an uncombed wig, and look rather dirty. M. Dolfin was not endowed with any of those eminent qualities, and therefore he had no hope of a great fortune in his native country.

The day before my departure from Venice I did not go out; I devoted the whole of the day to friendship. Madame Orio and her lovely nieces shed many tears, and I joined them in that delightful employment. During the last night that I spent with both of them, the sisters repeated over and over, in the midst of the raptures of love, that they never would see me again. They guessed rightly; but if they had happened to see me again they would have guessed wrongly. Observe how wonderful prophets are!

I went on board, on the 5th of May, with a good supply of clothing, jewels, and ready cash. Our ship carried twenty-four guns and two hundred Sclavonian soldiers. We sailed from Malamacca to the shores of Istria during the night, and we came to anchor in the harbour of Orsera to take ballast. I landed with several others to take a stroll through the wretched place where I had spent three days nine months before, a recollection which caused me a pleasant sensation when I compared my present position to what it was at that time. What a difference in everything—health, social condition, and money! I felt quite certain that in the splendid uniform I was now wearing nobody would recognize the miserable-looking abbe who, but for Friar Stephano, would have become—God knows what!

II

An Amusing Meeting in Orsera—Journey to Corfu—My
Stay in Constantinople—Bonneval—My Return to Corfu—
Madame F.—The False Prince—I Run Away from Corfu—My
Frolics at Casopo—I Surrender My self a Prisoner—My
Speedy Release and Triumph—My Success with Madame F.

I affirm that a stupid servant is more dangerous than a bad one, and a
much greater plague, for one can be on one's guard against a wicked
person, but never against a fool. You can punish wickedness but not
stupidity, unless you send away the fool, male or female, who is guilty
of it, and if you do so you generally find out that the change has only
thrown you out of the frying-pan into the fire.

This chapter and the two following ones were written; they gave at
full length all the particulars which I must now abridge, for my silly
servant has taken the three chapters for her own purposes. She pleaded
as an excuse that the sheets of paper were old, written upon, covered
with scribbling and erasures, and that she had taken them in preference
to nice, clean paper, thinking that I would care much more for the last
than for the first. I flew into a violent passion, but I was wrong, for the
poor girl had acted with a good intent; her judgment alone had misled
her. It is well known that the first result of anger is to deprive the angry
man of the faculty of reason, for anger and reason do not belong to the
same family. Luckily, passion does not keep me long under its sway:
'Irasci, celerem tamen et placabilem esse'. After I had wasted my time
in hurling at her bitter reproaches, the force of which did not strike
her, and in proving to her that she was a stupid fool, she refuted all my
arguments by the most complete silence. There was nothing to do but
to resign myself, and, although not yet in the best of tempers, I went to
work. What I am going to write will probably not be so good as what I
had composed when I felt in the proper humour, but my readers must
be satisfied with it they will, like the engineer, gain in time what they
lose in strength.

I landed at Orsera while our ship was taking ballast, as a ship cannot
sail well when she is too light, and I was walking about when I remarked
a man who was looking at me very attentively. As I had no dread of any
creditor, I thought that he was interested by my fine appearance; I could

not find fault with such a feeling, and kept walking on, but as I passed him, he addressed me:

"Might I presume to enquire whether this is your first visit to Orsera, captain?"

"No, sir, it is my second visit to this city."

"Were you not here last year?"

"I was."

"But you were not in uniform then?"

"True again; but your questions begin to sound rather indiscreet."

"Be good enough to forgive me, sir, for my curiosity is the offspring of gratitude. I am indebted to you for the greatest benefits, and I trust that Providence has brought you here again only to give me the opportunity of making greater still my debt of gratitude to you."

"What on earth have I done, and what can I do for you? I am at a loss to guess your meaning."

"Will you be so kind as to come and breakfast with me? My house is near at hand; my refosco is delicious, please to taste it, and I will convince you in a few words that you are truly my benefactor, and that I have a right to expect that you have returned Orsera to load me with fresh benefits."

I could not suspect the man of insanity; but, as I could not make him out, I fancied that he wanted to make me purchase some of his refosco, and I accepted his invitation. We went up to his room, and he left me for a few moments to order breakfast. I observed several surgical instruments, which made me suppose that he was a surgeon, and I asked him when he returned.

"Yes, captain; I have been practising surgery in this place for twenty years, and in a very poor way, for I had nothing to do, except a few cases of bleeding, of cupping, and occasionally some slight excoriation to dress or a sprained ankle to put to rights. I did not earn even the poorest living. But since last year a great change has taken place; I have made a good deal of money, I have laid it out advantageously, and it is to you, captain, to you (may God bless you!) that I am indebted for my present comforts."

"But how so?"

"In this way, captain. You had a connection with Don Jerome's housekeeper, and you left her, when you went away, a certain souvenir which she communicated to a friend of hers, who, in perfect good faith, made a present of it to his wife. This lady did not wish, I suppose, to be selfish, and she gave the souvenir to a libertine who, in his turn, was so generous with it that, in less than a month, I had about fifty clients. The following months were not less fruitful, and I gave the benefit of my attendance to everybody, of course, for a consideration. There are a few patients still under my care, but in a short time there will be no more, as the souvenir left by you has now lost all its virtue. You can easily realize now the joy I felt when I saw you; you are a bird of good omen. May I hope that your visit will last long enough to enable you to renew the source of my fortune?"

I laughed heartily, but he was grieved to hear that I was in excellent health. He remarked, however, that I was not likely to be so well off on my return, because, in the country to which I was going, there was abundance of damaged goods, but that no one knew better than he did how to root out the venom left by the use of such bad merchandise. He begged that I would depend upon him, and not trust myself in the hands of quacks, who would be sure to palm their remedies upon me. I promised him everything, and, taking leave of him with many thanks, I returned to the ship. I related the whole affair to M. Dolfin, who was highly amused. We sailed on the following day, but on the fourth day, on the other side of Curzola, we were visited by a storm which very nearly cost me my life. This is how it happened:

The chaplain of the ship was a Sclavonian priest, very ignorant, insolent and coarse-mannered, and, as I turned him into ridicule whenever the opportunity offered, he had naturally become my sworn enemy. 'Tant de fiel entre-t-il dans l'ame d'un devot!' When the storm was at its height, he posted himself on the quarter-deck, and, with book in hand, proceeded to exorcise all the spirits of hell whom he thought he could see in the clouds, and to whom he pointed for the benefit of the sailors who, believing themselves lost, were crying, howling, and giving way to despair, instead of attending to the working of the ship, then in great danger on account of the rocks and of the breakers which surrounded us.

Seeing the peril of our position, and the evil effect of his stupid, incantations upon the minds of the sailors whom the ignorant priest was throwing into the apathy of despair, instead of keeping up their courage, I thought it prudent to interfere. I went up the rigging, calling upon the sailors to do their duty cheerfully, telling them that there were no devils, and that the priest who pretended to see them was a fool. But it was in vain that I spoke in the most forcible manner, in vain that

I went to work myself, and shewed that safety was only to be insured by active means, I could not prevent the priest declaring that I was an Atheist, and he managed to rouse against me the anger of the greatest part of the crew. The wind continued to lash the sea into fury for the two following days, and the knave contrived to persuade the sailors who listened to him that the hurricane would not abate as long as I was on board. Imbued with that conviction, one of the men, thinking he had found a good opportunity of fulfilling the wishes of the priest, came up to me as I was standing at the extreme end of the forecastle, and pushed me so roughly that I was thrown over. I should have been irretrievably lost, but the sharp point of an anchor, hanging along the side of the ship, catching in my clothes, prevented me from falling in the sea, and proved truly my sheet-anchor. Some men came to my assistance, and I was saved. A corporal then pointed out to me the sailor who had tried to murder me, and taking a stout stick I treated the scoundrel to a sound thrashing; but the sailors, headed by the furious priest, rushed towards us when they heard his screams, and I should have been killed if the soldiers had not taken my part. The commander and M. Dolfin then came on deck, but they were compelled to listen to the chaplain, and to promise, in order to pacify the vile rabble, that they would land me at the first opportunity. But even this was not enough; the priest demanded that I should give up to him a certain parchment that I had purchased from a Greek at Malamocco just before sailing. I had no recollection of it, but it was true. I laughed, and gave it to M. Dolfin; he handed it to the fanatic chaplain, who, exulting in his victory, called for a large pan of live coals from the cook's galley, and made an auto-da-fe of the document. The unlucky parchment, before it was entirely consumed, kept writhing on the fire for half an hour, and the priest did not fail to represent those contortions as a miracle, and all the sailors were sure that it was an infernal manuscript given to me by the devil. The virtue claimed for that piece of parchment by the man who had sold it to me was that it insured its lucky possessor the love of all women, but I trust my readers will do me the justice to believe that I had no faith whatever in amorous philtres, talismans, or amulets of any kind: I had purchased it only for a joke.

You can find throughout Italy, in Greece, and generally in every country the inhabitants of which are yet wrapped up in primitive ignorance, a tribe of Greeks, of Jews, of astronomers, and of exorcists, who sell their dupes rags and toys to which they boastingly attach wonderful virtues and properties; amulets which render invulnerable, scraps of cloth which defend from witchcraft, small bags filled with drugs to keep away goblins, and a thousand gewgaws of the same description. These wonderful goods have no marketable value whatever in France, in England, in Germany, and throughout the north of Europe generally, but, in revenge, the inhabitants of those countries indulge in knavish practices of a much worse kind.

The storm abated just as the innocent parchment was writhing on the fire, and the sailors, believing that the spirits of hell had been exorcised, thought no more of getting rid of my person, and after a prosperous voyage of a week we cast anchor at Corfu. As soon as I had found a comfortable lodging I took my letters to his eminence the proveditore-generale, and to all the naval commanders to whom I was recommended; and after paying my respects to my colonel, and making the acquaintance of the officers of my regiment, I prepared to enjoy myself until the arrival of the Chevalier Venier, who had promised to take me to Constantinople. He arrived towards the middle of June, but in the mean time I had been playing basset, and had lost all my money, and sold or pledged all my jewellery.

Such must be the fate awaiting every man who has a taste for gambling, unless he should know how to fix fickle fortune by playing with a real advantage derived from calculation or from adroitness, which defies chance. I think that a cool and prudent player can manage both without exposing himself to censure, or deserving to be called a cheat.

During the month that I spent in Corfu, waiting for the arrival of M. Venier, I did not devote any time to the study, either moral or physical, of the country, for, excepting the days on which I was on duty, I passed my life at the coffee-house, intent upon the game, and sinking, as a matter of course, under the adverse fortune which I braved with obstinacy. I never won, and I had not the moral strength to stop till all my means were gone. The only comfort I had, and a sorry one truly, was to hear the banker himself call me—perhaps sarcastically—a fine player, every time I lost a large stake. My misery was at its height, when new life was infused in me by the booming of the guns fired in honour of the arrival of the bailo. He was on board the Europa, a frigate of seventy-two guns, and he had taken only eight days to sail from Venice to Corfu. The moment he cast anchor, the bailo hoisted his flag of captain-general of the Venetian navy, and the proveditore hauled down his own colours. The Republic of Venice has not on the sea any authority greater than that of Bailo to the Porte. The

Chevalier Venier had with him a distinguished and brilliant suite; Count Annibal Gambera, Count Charles Zenobio, both Venetian noblemen of the first class, and the Marquis d'Anchotti of Bressan, accompanied him to Constantinople for their own amusement. The bailo remained a week in Corfu, and all the naval authorities entertained him and his suite in turn, so that there was a constant succession of balls and suppers. When I presented myself to his excellency, he informed me that he had already spoken to the proveditore, who had granted me a furlough of six months to enable me to accompany him to Constantinople as his adjutant; and as soon as the official document for my furlough had been delivered to me, I sent my small stock of worldly goods on board the Europa, and we weighed anchor early the next day.

We sailed with a favourable wind which remained steady and brought us in six days to Cerigo, where we stopped to take in some water. Feeling some curiosity to visit the ancient Cythera, I went on shore with the sailors on duty, but it would have been better for me if I had remained on board, for in Cerigo I made a bad acquaintance. I was accompanied by the captain of marines.

The moment we set foot on shore, two men, very poorly dressed and of unprepossessing appearance, came to us and begged for assistance. I asked them who they were, and one, quicker than the other, answered;

"We are sentenced to live, and perhaps to die, in this island by the despotism of the Council of Ten. There are forty others as unfortunate as ourselves, and we are all born subjects of the Republic.

"The crime of which we have been accused, which is not considered a crime anywhere, is that we were in the habit of living with our mistresses, without being jealous of our friends, when, finding our ladies handsome, they obtained their favours with our ready consent. As we were not rich, we felt no remorse in availing ourselves of the generosity of our friends in such cases, but it was said that we were carrying on an illicit trade, and we have been sent to this place, where we receive every day ten sous in 'moneta lunga'. We are called 'mangia-mayroni', and are worse off than galley slaves, for we are dying of ennui, and we are often starving without knowing how to stay our hunger. My name is Don Antonio Pocchini, I am of a noble Paduan family, and my mother belongs to the illustrious family of Campo San-Piero."

We gave them some money, and went about the island, returning to the ship after we had visited the fortress. I shall have to speak of that Pocchini in a few years.

The wind continued in our favour, and we reached the Dardanelles in eight or ten days; the Turkish barges met us there to carry us to Constantinople. The sight offered by that city at the distance of a league is truly wonderful; and I believe that a more magnificent panorama cannot be found in any part of the world. It was that splendid view which was the cause of the fall of the Roman, and of the rise of the Greek empire. Constantine the Great, arriving at Byzantium by sea, was so much struck with the wonderful beauty of its position, that he exclaimed, "Here is the proper seat of the empire of the whole world!" and in order to secure the fulfilment of his prediction, he left Rome for Byzantium. If he had known the prophecy of Horace, or rather if he had believed in it, he would not have been guilty of such folly. The poet had said that the downfall of the Roman empire would begin only when one of the successors of Augustus bethought him removing the capital of the empire to where it had originated. The road is not far distant from Thrace.

We arrived at the Venetian Embassy in Pera towards the middle of July, and, for a wonder, there was no talk of the plague in Constantinople just then. We were all provided with very comfortable lodgings, but the intensity of the heat induced the baili to seek for a little coolness in a country mansion which had been hired by the Bailo Dona. It was situated at Bouyoudere. The very first order laid upon me was never to go out unknown to the bailo, and without being escorted by a janissary, and this order I obeyed to the letter. In those days the Russians had not tamed the insolence of the Turkish people. I am told that foreigners can now go about as much as they please in perfect security.

The day after our arrival, I took a janissary to accompany me to Osman Pacha, of Caramania, the name assumed by Count de Bonneval ever since he had adopted the turban. I sent in my letter, and was immediately shewn into an apartment on the ground floor, furnished in the French fashion, where I saw a stout elderly gentleman, dressed like a Frenchman, who, as I entered the room, rose, came to meet me with a smiling countenance, and asked me how he could serve the 'protege' of a cardinal of the Roman Catholic Church, which he could no longer call his mother. I gave him all the particulars of the circumstances which, in a moment of despair, had induced me to ask the cardinal for letters of introduction for Constantinople, and I added that, the letters once in my possession, my superstitious feelings had made me believe that I was bound to deliver them in person.

"Then, without this letter," he said, "you never would have come to Constantinople, and you have no need of me?"

"True, but I consider myself fortunate in having thus made the acquaintance of a man who has attracted the attention of the whole of Europe, and who still commands that attention."

His excellency made some remark respecting the happiness of young men who, like me, without care, without any fixed purpose, abandon themselves to fortune with that confidence which knows no fear, and telling me that the cardinal's letter made it desirable that he should do something for me, he promised to introduce me to three or four of his Turkish friends who deserved to be known. He invited me to dine with him every Thursday, and undertook to send me a janissary who would protect me from the insults of the rabble and shew me everything worth seeing.

The cardinal's letter representing me as a literary man, the pacha observed that I ought to see his library. I followed him through the garden, and we entered a room furnished with grated cupboards; curtains could be seen behind the wirework; the books were most likely behind the curtains.

Taking a key out of his pocket, he opened one of the cupboards, and, instead of folios, I saw long rows of bottles of the finest wines. We both laughed heartily.

"Here are," said the pacha, "my library and my harem. I am old, women would only shorten my life but good wine will prolong it, or at least, make it more agreeable.

"I imagine your excellency has obtained a dispensation from the mufti?"

"You are mistaken, for the Pope of the Turks is very far from enjoying as great a power as the Christian Pope. He cannot in any case permit what is forbidden by the Koran; but everyone is at liberty to work out his own damnation if he likes. The Turkish devotees pity the libertines, but they do not persecute them; there is no inquisition in Turkey. Those who do not know the precepts of religion, say the Turks, will suffer enough in the life to come; there is no need to make them suffer in this life. The only dispensation I have asked and obtained, has been respecting circumcision, although it can hardly be called so, because, at my age, it might have proved dangerous. That ceremony is generally performed, but it is not compulsory."

During the two hours that we spent together, the pacha enquired after several of his friends in Venice, and particularly after Marc

Antonio Dieto. I told him that his friends were still faithful to their affection for him, and did not find fault with his apostasy. He answered that he was a Mahometan as he had been a Christian, and that he was not better acquainted with the Koran than he had been with the Gospel. "I am certain," he added, "that I shall die-calmer and much happier than Prince Eugene. I have had to say that God is God, and that Mahomet is the prophet. I have said it, and the Turks care very little whether I believe it or not. I wear the turban as the soldier wears the uniform. I was nothing but a military man; I could not have turned my hand to any other profession, and I made up my mind to become lieutenant-general of the Grand Turk only when I found myself entirely at a loss how to earn my living. When I left Venice, the pitcher had gone too often to the well, it was broken at last, and if the Jews had offered me the command of an army of fifty thousand men, I would have gone and besieged Jerusalem."

Bonneval was handsome, but too stout. He had received a sabre-cut in the lower part of the abdomen, which compelled him to wear constantly a bandage supported by a silver plate. He had been exiled to Asia, but only for a short time, for, as he told me, the cabals are not so tenacious in Turkey as they are in Europe, and particularly at the court of Vienna. As I was taking leave of him, he was kind enough to say that, since his arrival in Turkey, he had never passed two hours as pleasantly as those he had just spent with me, and that he would compliment the bailo about me.

The Bailo Dona, who had known him intimately in Venice, desired me to be the bearer of all his friendly compliments for him, and M. Venier expressed his deep regret at not being able to make his acquaintance.

The second day after my first visit to him being a Thursday, the pacha did not forget to send a janissary according to his promise. It was about eleven in the morning when the janissary called for me, I followed him, and this time I found Bonneval dressed in the Turkish style. His guests soon arrived, and we sat down to dinner, eight of us, all well disposed to be cheerful and happy. The dinner was entirely French, in cooking and service; his steward and his cook were both worthy French renegades.

He had taken care to introduce me to all his guests and at the same time to let me know who they were, but he did not give me an opportunity of speaking before dinner was nearly over. The conversation was entirely kept up in Italian, and I remarked that the Turks did not utter a single word in their own language, even to say the most ordinary thing. Each guest had near him a bottle which might have contained either white wine or hydromel; all I know is that I drank, as well as M. de Bonneval, next to whom I was seated, some excellent white Burgundy.

The guests got me on the subject of Venice, and particularly of Rome, and the conversation very naturally fell upon religion, but not upon dogmatic questions; the discipline of religion and liturgical questions were alone discussed.

One of the guests, who was addressed as effendi, because he had been secretary for foreign affairs, said that the ambassador from Venice to Rome was a friend of his, and he spoke of him in the highest manner. I told him that I shared his admiration for that ambassador, who had given me a letter of introduction for a Turkish nobleman, whom he had represented as an intimate friend. He enquired for the name of the person to whom the letter was addressed, but I could not recollect it, and took the letter out of my pocket-book. The effendi was delighted when he found that the letter was for himself. He begged leave to read it at once, and after he had perused it, he kissed the signature and came to embrace me. This scene pleased M. de Bonneval and all his friends. The effendi, whose name was Ismail, entreated the pacha to come to dine with him, and to bring me; Bonneval accepted, and fixed a day.

Notwithstanding all the politeness of the effendi, I was particularly interested during our charming dinner in a fine elderly man of about sixty, whose countenance breathed at the same time the greatest sagacity and the most perfect kindness. Two years afterwards I found again the same features on the handsome face of M. de Bragadin, a Venetian senator of whom I shall have to speak at length when we come to that period of my life. That elderly gentleman had listened to me with the greatest attention, but without uttering one word. In society, a man whose face and general appearance excite your interest, stimulates strongly your curiosity if he remains silent. When we left the dining-room I enquired from de Bonneval who he was; he answered that he was wealthy, a philosopher, a man of acknowledged merit, of great purity of morals, and strongly attached to his religion. He advised me to cultivate his acquaintance if he made any advances to me.

I was pleased with his advice, and when, after a walk under the shady trees of the garden, we returned to a drawing-room furnished in the Turkish fashion, I purposely took a seat near Yusuf Ali. Such was the name of the Turk for whom I felt so much sympathy. He offered me his pipe in a very graceful manner; I refused it politely, and took one brought to me by one of M. de Bonneval's servants. Whenever I have been amongst smokers I have smoked or left the room; otherwise I would have fancied that I was swallowing the smoke of the others, and that idea which is true and unpleasant, disgusted me. I have never been able to understand how in Germany the ladies, otherwise so polite and delicate, could inhale the suffocating fumes of a crowd of smokers.

Yusuf, pleased to have me near him, at once led the conversation to subjects similar to those which had been discussed at table, and particularly to the reasons which had induced me to give up the peaceful profession of the Church and to choose a military life; and in order to gratify his curiosity without losing his good opinion, I gave him, but with proper caution, some of the particulars of my life, for I wanted him to be satisfied that, if I had at first entered the career of the holy priesthood, it had not been through any vocation of mine. He seemed pleased with my recital, spoke of natural vocations as a Stoic philosopher, and I saw that he was a fatalist; but as I was careful not to attack his system openly, he did not dislike my objections, most likely because he thought himself strong enough to overthrow them.

I must have inspired the honest Mussulman with very great esteem, for he thought me worthy of becoming his disciple; it was not likely that he could entertain the idea of becoming himself the disciple of a young man of nineteen, lost, as he thought, in a false religion.

After spending an hour in examining me, in listening to my principles, he said that he believed me fit to know the real truth, because he saw that I was seeking for it, and that I was not certain of having obtained it so far. He invited me to come and spend a whole day with him, naming the days when I would be certain to find him at home, but he advised me to consult the Pacha Osman before accepting his invitation. I told him that the pacha had already mentioned him to me and had spoken very highly of his character; he seemed much pleased. I fixed a day for my visit, and left him.

I informed M. de Bonneval of all that had occurred; he was delighted, and promised that his janissary would be every day at the Venetian palace, ready to execute my orders.

I received the congratulations of the baili upon the excellent acquaintances I had already made, and M. Venier advised me not to neglect such friends in a country where weariness of life was more deadly to foreigners than the plague.

On the day appointed, I went early to Yusuf's palace, but he was out. His gardener, who had received his instructions, shewed me every attention, and entertained me very agreeably for two hours in doing the honours of his master's splendid garden, where I found the most beautiful flowers. This gardener was a Neapolitan, and had belonged to Yusuf for thirty years. His manners made me suspect that he was well born and well educated, but he told me frankly that he had never been taught even to read, that he was a sailor when he, was taken in slavery, and that he was so happy in the service of Yusuf that liberty would be a punishment to him. Of course I did not venture to address him any questions about his master, for his reserve might have put my curiosity to the blush.

Yusuf had gone out on horseback; he returned, and, after the usual compliments, we dined alone in a summerhouse, from which we had a fine view of the sea, and in which the heat was cooled by a delightful breeze, which blows regularly at the same hour every day from the north-west; and is called the mistral. We had a good dinner; there was no prepared dish except the cauroman, a peculiar delicacy of the Turks. I drank water and hydromel, and I told Yusuf that I preferred the last to wine, of which I never took much at that time. "Your hydromel," I said, "is very good, and the Mussulmans who offend against the law by drinking wine do not deserve any indulgence; I believe they drink wine only because it is forbidden." "Many of the true believers," he answered, "think that they can take it as a medicine. The Grand Turk's physician has brought it into vogue as a medicine, and it has been the cause of his fortune, for he has captivated the favour of his master who is in reality constantly ill, because he is always in a state of intoxication." I told Yusuf that in my country drunkards were scarce, and that drunkenness was a vice to be found only among the lowest people; he was much astonished. "I cannot understand," he said, "why wine is allowed by all religions, when its use deprives man of his reason."—"All religions," I answered, "forbid excess in drinking wine, and the crime is only in the abuse." I proved him the truth of what I had said by telling him that opium produced the same results as wine, but more powerfully, and consequently Mahomet ought to have forbidden the use of it. He observed that he had never taken either wine or opium in the course of his life.

After dinner, pipes were brought in and we filled them ourselves. I was smoking with pleasure, but, at the same time, was expectorating. Yusuf, who smoked like a Turk, that is to say, without spitting, said,—

"The tobacco you are now smoking is of a very fine quality, and you ought to swallow its balsam which is mixed with the saliva."

"I suppose you are right; smoking cannot be truly enjoyed without the best tobacco."

"That is true to a certain extent, but the enjoyment found in smoking good tobacco is not the principal pleasure, because it only pleases our senses; true enjoyment is that which works upon the soul, and is completely independent of the senses."

"I cannot realize pleasures enjoyed by the soul without the instrumentality of the senses."

"Listen to me. When you fill your pipe do you feel any pleasure?"

"Yes."

"Whence does that pleasure arise, if it is not from your soul? Let us go further. Do you not feel pleased when you give up your pipe after having smoked all the tobacco in it—when you see that nothing is left but some ashes?"

"It is true."

"Well, there are two pleasures in which your senses have certainly nothing to do, but I want you to guess the third, and the most essential."

"The most essential? It is the perfume."

"No; that is a pleasure of the organ of smelling—a sensual pleasure."

"Then I do not know."

"Listen. The principal pleasure derived from tobacco smoking is the sight of a smoke itself. You must never see it go out of the bowl of your pipe,—but only from the corner o your mouth, at regular intervals which must not be too frequent. It is so truly the greatest pleasure connected with the pipe, that you cannot find anywhere a blind man who smokes. Try yourself the experiment of smoking a pipe in your room, at night and without a light; you will soon lay the pipe down."

"It is all perfectly true; yet you must forgive me if I give the preference to several pleasures, in which my senses are interested, over those which afford enjoyment only to my soul."

"Forty years ago I was of the same opinion, and in forty years, if you succeed in acquiring wisdom, you will think like me. Pleasures which give activity to our senses, my dear son, disturb the repose of our soul—a proof that they do not deserve the name of real enjoyments."

"But if I feel them to be real enjoyments, it is enough to prove that they are truly so."

"Granted; but if you would take the trouble of analyzing them after you have tasted them, you would not find them unalloyed."

"It may be so, but why should I take a trouble which would only lessen my enjoyment."

"A time will come when you will feel pleasure in that very trouble."

"It strikes me, dear father, that you prefer mature age to youth."

"You may boldly say old age."

"You surprise me. Must I believe that your early life has been unhappy?"

"Far from it. It was always fortunate in good health, and the master of my own passions; but all I saw in my equals was for me a good school in which I have acquired the knowledge of man, and learned the real road to happiness. The happiest of men is not the most voluptuous, but the one who knows how to choose the highest standards of voluptuousness, which can be found, I say again, not in the pleasures which excite our senses, but in those which give greater repose to the soul."

"That is the voluptuousness which you consider unalloyed."

"Yes, and such is the sight of a vast prairie all covered with grass. The green colour, so strongly recommended by our divine prophet, strikes my eyes, and at the same moment I feel that my soul is wrapped up in a calm so delightful that I fancy myself nearer the Creator. I enjoy the same peace, the same repose, when I am seated on the banks of a river, when I look upon the water so quiet, yet always moving, which flows constantly, yet never disappears from my sight, never loses any of its clearness in spite of its constant motion. It strikes me as the image of my own existence, and of the calm which I require for my life in order to reach, like the water I am gazing upon, the goal which I do not see, and which can only be found at the other end of the journey."

Thus did the Turk reason, and we passed four hours in this sort of conversation. He had buried two wives, and he had two sons and one daughter. The eldest son, having received his patrimony, had established himself in the city of Salonica, where he was a wealthy merchant; the other was in the seraglio, in the service of the Grand Turk and his fortune was in the hands of a trustee. His daughter, Zelmi, then fifteen years of age, was to inherit all his remaining property. He had given her all the accomplishments which could minister to the happiness of the man whom heaven had destined for her husband. We shall hear more of that daughter anon. The mother of the three children was dead, and five years previous to the time of my visit, Yusuf had taken another wife, a native of Scio, young and very beautiful, but he told me himself that he was now too old, and could not hope to have any child by her. Yet he was only sixty years of age. Before I left, he made me promise to spend at least one day every week with him.

At supper, I told the baili how pleasantly the day had passed.

"We envy you," they said, "the prospect you have before you of spending agreeably three or four months in this country, while, in our quality of ministers, we must pine away with melancholy."

A few days afterwards, M. de Bonneval took me with him to dine at Ismail's house, where I saw Asiatic luxury on a grand scale, but there were a great many guests, and the conversation was held almost entirely in the Turkish language—a circumstance which annoyed me and M. de Bonneval also. Ismail saw it, and he invited me to breakfast whenever I felt disposed, assuring me that he would have much pleasure in receiving me. I accepted the invitation, and I went ten or twelve days afterwards. When we reach that period my readers must kindly accompany me to the breakfast. For the present I must return to Yusuf who, during my second visit, displayed a character which inspired, me with the greatest esteem and the warmest affection.

We had dined alone as before, and, conversation happening to turn upon the fine arts, I gave my opinion upon one of the precepts in the Koran, by which the Mahometans are deprived of the innocent enjoyment of paintings and statues. He told me that Mahomet, a very sagacious legislator, had been right in removing all images from the sight of the followers of Islam.

"Recollect, my son, that the nations to which the prophet brought the knowledge of the true God were all idolators. Men are weak; if the disciples of the prophet had continued to see the same objects, they might have fallen back into their former errors."

"No one ever worshipped an image as an image; the deity of which the image is a representation is what is worshipped."

"I may grant that, but God cannot be matter, and it is right to remove from the thoughts of the vulgar the idea of a material divinity. You are the only men, you Christians, who believe that you see God."

"It is true, we are sure of it, but observe that faith alone gives us that certainty."

"I know it; but you are idolators, for you see nothing but a material representation, and yet you have a complete certainty that you see God, unless you should tell me that faith disaffirms it."

GIACOMO CASANOVA

"God forbid I should tell you such a thing! Faith, on the contrary, affirms our certainty."

"We thank God that we have no need of such self-delusion, and there is not one philosopher in the world who could prove to me that you require it."

"That would not be the province of philosophy, dear father, but of theology—a very superior science."

"You are now speaking the language of our theologians, who differ from yours only in this; they use their science to make clearer the truths we ought to know, whilst your theologians try to render those truths more obscure."

"Recollect, dear father, that they are mysteries."

"The existence of God is a sufficiently important mystery to prevent men from daring to add anything to it. God can only be simple; any kind of combination would destroy His essence; such is the God announced by our prophet, who must be the same for all men and in all times. Agree with me that we can add nothing to the simplicity of God. We say that God is one; that is the image of simplicity. You say that He is one and three at the same time, and such a definition strikes us as contradictory, absurd, and impious."

"It is a mystery."

"Do you mean God or the definition? I am speaking only of the definition, which ought not to be a mystery or absurd. Common sense, my son, must consider as absurd an assertion which substantially nonsensical. Prove to me that three is not a compound, that it cannot be a compound and I will become a Christian at once."

"My religion tells me to believe without arguing, and I shudder, my dear Yusuf, when I think that, through some specious reasoning, I might be led to renounce the creed of my fathers. I first must be convinced that they lived in error. Tell me whether, respecting my father's memory, I ought to have such a good opinion of myself as to sit in judgement over him, with the intention of giving my sentence against him?"

My lively remonstrance moved Yusuf deeply, but after a few instants of silence he said to me,—

"With such feelings, my son, you are sure to find grace in the eyes of God, and you are, therefore, one of the elect. If you are in error, God alone can convince you of it, for no just man on earth can refute the sentiment you have just given expression to."

We spoke of many other things in a friendly manner, and in the evening we parted with the often repeated assurance of the warmest affection and of the most perfect devotion.

But my mind was full of our conversation, and as I went on pondering over the matter, I thought that Yusuf might be right in his opinion as to the essence of God, for it seemed evident that the Creator of all beings ought to be perfectly simple; but I thought at the same time how impossible it would be for me, because the Christian religion had made a mistake, to accept the Turkish creed, which might perhaps have just a conception of God, but which caused me to smile when I recollected that the man who had given birth to it had been an arrant imposter. I had not the slightest idea, however, that Yusuf wished to make a convert of me.

The third time I dined with him religion was again the subject of conversation.

"Do you believe, dear father, that the religion of Mahomet is the only one in which salvation can be secured?"

"No, my dear son, I am not certain of it, and no man can have such a certainty; but I am sure that the Christian religion is not the true one, because it cannot be universal."

"Why not?"

"Because there is neither bread nor wine to be found in three-fourths of the world. Observe that the precepts of the Koran can be followed everywhere."

I did not know how to answer, and I would not equivocate.

"If God cannot be matter," I said, "then He must be a spirit?"

"We know what He is not but we do not know what He is: man cannot affirm that God is a spirit, because he can only realize the idea in an abstract manner. God immaterial; that is the extent of our knowledge and it can never be greater."

I was reminded of Plato, who had said exactly the same an most certainly Yusuf never read Plato.

He added that the existence of God could be useful only to those who did not entertain a doubt of that existence, and that, as a natural consequence, Atheists must be the most miserable of men. God has made in man His own image in order that, amongst all the animals created by Him, there should be one that can understand and confess the existence of the Creator. Without man, God would have no witness of His own glory, and man must therefore understand that his first and highest duty is to glorify God by practising justice and trusting to His providence.

"Observe, my son, that God never abandons the man who, in the midst of misfortunes, falls down in prayer before Him, and that He often allows the wretch who has no faith in prayer to die miserably."

"Yet we meet with Atheists who are fortunate and happy."

"True; but, in spite of their tranquillity, I pity them because they have no hope beyond this life, and are on a level with animals. Besides, if they are philosophers, they must linger in dark ignorance, and, if they never think, they have no consolation, no resource, when adversity reaches them. God has made man in such a manner that he cannot be happy unless he entertains no doubt of the existence of his Divine Creator; in all stations of life man is naturally prone to believe in that existence, otherwise man would never have admitted one God, Creator of all beings and of all things."

"I should like to know why Atheism has only existed in the systems of the learned, and never as a national creed."

"Because the poor feel their wants much more than the rich, There are amongst us a great many impious men who deride the true believers because they have faith in the pilgrimage to Mecca. Wretches that they are, they ought to respect the ancient customs which, exciting the devotion of fervent souls, feed religious principles, and impart courage under all misfortunes. Without such consolation, people would give way to all the excess of despair."

Much pleased with the attention I gave to all he said, Yusuf would thus yield to the inclination he felt to instruct me, and, on my side, feeling myself drawn towards him by the charm which amiable goodness exerts upon all hearts, I would often go and spend the day with him, even without any previous invitation, and Yusuf's friendship soon became one of my most precious treasures.

One morning, I told my janissary to take me to the palace of Ismail Effendi, in order to fulfil my promise to breakfast with him. He gave me the most friendly welcome, and after an excellent breakfast he invited me to take a walk in his garden. We found there a pretty summer-house which we entered, and Ismail attempted some liberties which were not at all to my taste, and which I resented by rising in a very abrupt manner. Seeing that I was angry, the Turk affected to approve my reserve, and said that he had only been joking. I left him after a few minutes, with the intention of not visiting him again, but I was compelled to do so, as I will explain by-and-by.

When I saw M. de Bonneval I told him what had happened and he said that, according to Turkish manners, Ismail had intended to give me a great proof of his friendship, but that I need not be afraid of the offence being repeated. He added that politeness required that I should visit him again, and that Ismail was, in spite of his failing, a perfect gentleman, who had at his disposal the most beautiful female slaves in Turkey.

Five or six weeks after the commencement of our intimacy, Yusuf asked me one day whether I was married. I answered that I was not; the conversation turned upon several moral questions, and at last fell upon chastity, which, in his opinion, could be accounted a virtue only if considered from one point of view, namely, that of total abstinence, but he added that it could not be acceptable to God; because it transgressed against the very first precept He had given to man.

"I would like to know, for instance," he said, "what name can be given to the chastity of your knights of Malta. They take a vow of chastity, but it does not mean that they will renounce women altogether, they renounce marriage only. Their chastity, and therefore chastity in general, is violated only by marriage; yet I observe that marriage is one of your sacraments. Therefore, those knights of Malta promise not to give way to lustful incontinence in the only case in which God might forgive it, but they reserve the license of being lustful unlawfully as often as they please, and whenever an opportunity may offer itself; and that immoral, illicit license is granted to them to such an extent, that they are allowed to acknowledge legally a child which can be born to them only through a double crime! The most revolting part of it all is that these children of crime, who are of course perfectly innocent themselves, are called natural children, as if children born in wedlock came into the world in an unnatural manner! In one word, my dear son, the vow of chastity is so much opposed to Divine precepts and to human nature that it can be agreeable neither to God nor to society, nor to those who pledge themselves to keep it, and being in such opposition to every divine and human law, it must be a crime."

He enquired for the second time whether I was married; I replied in the negative, and added that I had no idea of ever getting married.

"What!" he exclaimed; "I must then believe that you are not a perfect man, or that you intend to work out your own damnation; unless you should tell me that you are a Christian only outwardly."

"I am a man in the very strongest sense of the word, and I am a true Christian. I must even confess that I adore women, and that I have not the slightest idea of depriving myself of the most delightful of all pleasures."

"According to your religion, damnation awaits you."

"I feel certain of the contrary, because, when we confess our sins, our priests are compelled to give us absolution."

"I know it, but you must agree with me that it is absurd to suppose that God will forgive a crime which you would, perhaps, not commit, if you did not think that, after confession, a priest, a man like you, will give you absolution. God forgives only the repenting sinner."

"No doubt of it, and confession supposes repentance; without it, absolution has no effect."

"Is onanism a crime amongst you?"

"Yes, even greater than lustful and illegitimate copulation."

"I was aware of it, and it has always caused me great surprise, for the legislator who enacts a law, the execution of which is impossible, is a fool. A man in good health, if he cannot have a woman, must necessarily have recourse to onanism, whenever imperious nature demands it, and the man who, from fear of polluting his soul, would abstain from it, would only draw upon himself a mortal disease."

"We believe exactly the reverse; we think that young people destroy their constitutions, and shorten their lives through self-abuse. In several communities they are closely watched, and are as much as possible deprived of every opportunity of indulging in that crime."

"Those who watch them are ignorant fools, and those who pay the watchers for such a service are even more stupid, because prohibition must excite the wish to break through such a tyrannical law, to set at nought an interdiction so contrary to nature."

"Yet it seems to me that self-abuse in excess must be injurious to health, for it must weaken and enervate."

"Certainly, because excess in everything is prejudicial and pernicious; but all such excess is the result of our severe prohibition. If girls are not interfered with in the matter of self-abuse, I do not see why boys should be."

"Because girls are very far from running the same risk; they do not lose a great deal in the action of self-abuse, and what they lose does not come from the same source whence flows the germinal liquid in men."

"I do not know, but we have some physicians who say that chlorosis in girls is the result of that pleasure indulged in to excess."

After many such conversations, in which he seemed to consider me as endowed with reason and talent, even when I was not of his opinion, Yusuf Ali surprised me greatly one day by the following proposition:

"I have two sons and a daughter. I no longer think of my sons, because they have received their share of my fortune. As far as my daughter is concerned she will, after my death, inherit all my possessions, and I am, besides, in a position while I am alive to promote the fortune of the man who may marry her. Five years ago I took a young wife, but she has not given me any progeny, and I know to a certainty that no offspring will bless our union. My daughter, whose name is Zelmi, is now fifteen; she is handsome, her eyes are black and lovely like her mother's, her hair is of the colour of the raven's wing, her complexion is animated alabaster; she is tall, well made, and of a sweet disposition; I have given her an education which would make her worthy of our master, the Sultan. She speaks Greek and Italian fluently, she sings delightfully, and accompanies herself on the harp; she can draw and embroider, and is always contented and cheerful. No living man can boast of having seen her features, and she loves me so dearly that my will is hers. My daughter is a treasure, and I offer her to you if you will consent to go for one year to Adrianople to reside with a relative of mine, who will teach you our religion, our language, and our manners. You will return at the end of one year, and as soon as you have become a Mussulman my daughter shall be your wife. You will find a house ready furnished, slaves of your own, and an income which will enable you to live in comfort. I have no more to say at present. I do not wish you to answer me either to-day, or to-morrow, or on any fixed day. You will give me your decision whenever you feel yourself called upon by your genius to give it, and you need not give me any answer unless you accept my offer, for, should you refuse it, it is not necessary that the subject should be again mentioned. I do not ask you to give full consideration to my proposal, for now that I have thrown the seed in your soul it must fructify. Without hurry, without delay, without anxiety, you can but obey the decrees of God and follow the immutable decision of fate. Such as I know you, I believe that you only require the possession of Zelmi to be completely happy, and that you will become one of the pillars of the Ottoman Empire."

Saying those words, Yusuf pressed me affectionately in his arms, and left me by myself to avoid any answer I might be inclined to make. I went away in such wonder at all I had just heard, that I found myself at the Venetian Embassy without knowing how I had reached it. The baili thought me very pensive, and asked whether anything was the matter with me, but I did not feel disposed to gratify their curiosity. I found that Yusuf had indeed spoken truly: his proposal was of such importance that it was my duty, not only not to mention it to anyone, but even to abstain from thinking it over, until my mind had recovered its calm sufficiently to give me the assurance that no external consideration would weigh in the balance and influence my decision. I had to silence all my passions; prejudices, principles already formed, love, and even self-interest were to remain in a state of complete inaction.

When I awoke the next morning I began to think the matter over, and I soon discovered that, if I wanted to come to a decision, I ought not to ponder over it, as the more I considered the less likely I should be to decide. This was truly a case for the 'sequere Deum' of the Stoics.

I did not visit Yusuf for four days, and when I called on him on the fifth day, we talked cheerfully without once mentioning his proposal, although it was very evident that we were both thinking of it. We remained thus for a fortnight, without ever alluding to the matter which engrossed all our thoughts, but our silence was not caused by dissimulation, or by any feeling contrary to our mutual esteem and friendship; and one day Yusuf suggested that very likely I had communicated his proposal to some wise friend, in order to obtain good advice. I immediately assured him it was not so, and that in a matter of so delicate a nature I thought I ought not to ask anybody's advice.

"I have abandoned myself to God, dear Yusuf, and, full of confidence in Him, I feel certain that I shall decide for the best, whether I make up my mind to become your son, or believe that I ought to remain what I am now. In the mean time, my mind ponders over it day and night, whenever I am quiet and feel myself composed and collected. When I come to a decision, I will impart it to you alone, and from that moment you shall have over me the authority of a father."

At these words the worthy Yusuf, his eyes wet with tears, placed his left hand over my head, and the first two fingers of the right hand on my forehead, saying:

"Continue to act in that way, my dear son, and be certain that you can never act wrongly."

"But," I said to him, "one thing might happen, Zelmi might not accept me."

"Have no anxiety about that. My daughter loves you; she, as well as my wife and her nurse, sees you every time that we dine together, and she listens to you with pleasure."

"Does she know that you are thinking of giving her to me as my wife?"

"She knows that I ardently wish you to become a true believer, so as to enable me to link her destiny to yours."

"I am glad that your habits do not permit you to let me see her, because she might dazzle me with her beauty, and then passion would soon have too much weight in the scale; I could no longer flatter myself that my decision had been taken in all the unbiased, purity of my soul."

Yusuf was highly delighted at hearing me speak in that manner, and I spoke in perfect good faith. The mere idea of seeing Zelmi caused me to shudder. I felt that, if I had fallen in love with her, I would have become a Mussulman in order to possess her, and that I might soon have repented such a step, for the religion of Mahomet presented to my eyes and to my mind nothing but a disagreeable picture, as well for this life as for a future one. As for wealth, I did not think it deserved the immense sacrifice demanded from me. I could find equal wealth in Europe, without stamping my forehead with the shameful brand of apostasy. I cared deeply for the esteem of the persons of distinction who knew me, and did not want to render myself unworthy of it. Besides, I felt an immense desire to obtain fame amongst civilized and polite nations, either in the fine arts or in literature, or in any other honourable profession, and I could not reconcile myself to the idea of abandoning to my equals the triumph which I might win if I lived amongst them. It seemed to me, and I am still of the same opinion, that the decision of wearing the turban befits only a Christian despairing of himself and at the end of his wits, and fortunately I was lost not in that predicament. My greatest objection was to spend a year in Adrianople to learn a language for which I did not feel any liking, and which I should therefore have learned but imperfectly. How could I, at my age, renounce the prerogative, so pleasant to my vanity, of being reputed a fine talker? and I had secured that reputation wherever I was known. Then I would often think that Zelmi, the eighth wonder of creation in the eyes of her father might not appear such in my eyes, and it would have been enough to make me miserable, for Yusuf was likely to live twenty years longer, and I felt that gratitude, as well as respect, would never have permitted me to give that excellent man any cause for unhappiness by ceasing to shew myself a devoted and faithful husband to his daughter. Such were my thoughts, and, as Yusuf could not guess them, it was useless to make a confidant of him.

A few days afterwards, I dined with the Pacha Osman and met my Effendi Ismail. He was very friendly to me, and I reciprocated his attentions, though I paid no attention to the reproaches he addressed to me for not having come to breakfast with him for such a long time. I could not refuse to dine at his house with Bonneval, and he treated me to a very pleasing sight; Neapolitan slaves, men and women, performed a pantomime and some Calabrian dances. M. de Bonneval happened to mention the dance called forlana, and Ismail expressing a great wish to know it, I told him that I could give him that pleasure if I had a Venetian woman to dance with and a fiddler who knew the time. I took a violin, and played the forlana, but, even if the partner had been found, I could not play and dance at the same time.

Ismail whispered a few words to one of his eunuchs, who went out of the room and returned soon with some message that he delivered to him. The effendi told me that he had found the partner I wanted, and I answered that the musician could be had easily, if he would send a note to the Venetian Embassy, which was done at once. The Bailo Dona sent one of his men who played the violin well enough for dancing purposes. As soon as the musician was ready, a door was thrown open, and a fine looking woman came in, her face covered with a black velvet mask, such as we call moretta in Venice. The appearance of that beautiful masked woman surprised and delighted every one of the guests, for it was impossible to imagine a more interesting object, not only on account of the beauty of that part of the face which the mask left exposed, but also for the elegance of her shape, the perfection of her figure, and the exquisite taste displayed in her costume. The nymph took her place, I did the same, and we danced the forlana six times without stopping.

I was in perspiration and out of breath, for the foylana is the most violent of our national dances; but my beautiful partner stood near me without betraying the slightest fatigue, and seemed to challenge me to a new performance. At the round of the dance, which is the most difficult step, she seemed to have wings. I was astounded, for I had never seen anyone, even in Venice, dance the forlana so splendidly. After a few minutes rest, rather ashamed of my feeling tired, I went up to her, and said, 'Ancora sei, a poi basta, se non volete vedermi a morire.' She would have answered me if she had been able, but she wore one of those cruel masks which forbid speech. But a pressure of her hand which nobody could see made me guess all I wanted to know. The moment we finished dancing the eunuch opened the door, and my lovely partner disappeared.

Ismail could not thank me enough, but it was I who owed him my thanks, for it was the only real pleasure which I enjoyed in Constantinople. I asked him whether the lady was from Venice, but he only answered by a significant smile.

"The worthy Ismail," said M. de Bonneval to me, as we were leaving the house late in the evening, "has been to-day the dupe of his vanity, and I have no doubt that he is sorry already for what he has done. To bring out his beautiful slave to dance with you! According to the prejudices of this country it is injurious to his dignity, for you are sure to have kindled an amorous flame in the poor girl's breast. I would advise you to be careful and to keep on your guard, because she will try to get up some intrigue with you; but be prudent, for intrigues are always dangerous in Turkey."

I promised to be prudent, but I did not keep my promise; for, three or four days afterwards, an old slave woman met me in the street, and offered to sell me for one piaster a tobacco-bag embroidered in gold; and as she put it in my hand she contrived to make me feel that there was a letter in the bag.

I observed that she tried to avoid the eyes of the janissary who was walking behind me; I gave her one piaster, she left me, and I proceeded toward Yusuf's house. He was not at home, and I went to his garden to read the letter with perfect freedom. It was sealed and without any address, and the slave might have made a mistake; but my curiosity was excited to the highest pitch; I broke the seal, and found the following note written in good enough Italian:

"Should you wish to see the person with whom you danced the forlana, take a walk towards evening in the garden beyond the fountain, and contrive to become acquainted with the old servant of the gardener by asking her for some lemonade. You may perchance manage to see your partner in the forlana without running any risk, even if you should happen to meet Ismail; she is a native of Venice. Be careful not to mention this invitation to any human being."

"I am not such a fool, my lovely countrywoman," I exclaimed, as if she had been present, and put the letter in my pocket. But at that very moment, a fine-looking elderly woman came out of a thicket, pronounced my name, and enquired what I wanted and how I had seen her. I answered that I had been speaking to the wind, not supposing that anyone could hear me, and without any more preparation, she abruptly told me that she was very glad of the opportunity of speaking with me, that she was from Rome, that she had brought up Zelmi, and had taught her to sing and to play the harp. She then praised highly the beauty and the excellent qualities of her pupil, saying that, if I saw her, I would certainly fall in love with her, and expressing how much she regretted that the law should not allow it.

"She sees us at this very moment," she added, "from behind that green window-blind, and we love you ever since Yusuf has informed us that you may, perhaps, become Zelmi's husband."

"May I mention our conversation to Yusuf?" I enquired.

"No."

Her answering in the negative made me understand that, if I had pressed her a little, she would have allowed me to see her lovely pupil, and perhaps it was with that intention that she had contrived to speak to me, but I felt great reluctance to do anything to displease my worthy host. I had another reason of even greater importance: I was afraid of entering an intricate maze in which the sight of a turban hovering over me made me shudder.

Yusuf came home, and far from being angry when he saw me with the woman, he remarked that I must have found much pleasure in conversing with a native of Rome, and he congratulated me upon the delight I must have felt in dancing with one of the beauties from the harem of the voluptuous Ismail.

"Then it must be a pleasure seldom enjoyed, if it is so much talked of?"

"Very seldom indeed, for there is amongst us an invincible prejudice against exposing our lovely women to the eyes of other men; but everyone may do as he pleases in his own house: Ismail is a very worthy and a very intelligent man."

"Is the lady with whom I danced known?"

"I believe not. She wore a mask, and everybody knows that Ismail possesses half a dozen slaves of surpassing beauty."

I spent a pleasant day with Yusuf, and when I left him, I ordered my janissary to take me to Ismail's. As I was known by his servants, they allowed me to go in, and I proceeded to the spot described in the letter. The eunuch came to me, informed me that his master was out, but that he would be delighted to hear of my having taken a walk in the garden.

I told him that I would like a glass of lemonade, and he took me to the summerhouse, where I recognized the old woman who had sold me the tobacco-pouch. The eunuch told her to give me a glass of some liquid which I found delicious, and would not allow me to give her any money. We then walked together towards the fountain, but he told me abruptly that we were to go back, as he saw three ladies to whom he pointed, adding that, for the sake of decency, it was necessary to avoid them. I thanked him for his attentions, left my compliments for Ismail, and went away not dissatisfied with my first attempt, and with the hope of being more fortunate another time.

The next morning I received a letter from Ismail inviting me to go fishing with him on the following day, and stating that he intended to enjoy the sport by moonlight. I immediately gave way to my suppositions, and I went so far as to fancy that Ismail might be capable of arranging an interview between me and the lovely Venetian. I did not mind his being present. I begged permission of Chevalier Venier to stop out of the palace for one night, but he granted it with the greatest difficulty, because he was afraid of some love affair and of the results it might have. I took care to calm his anxiety as much as I could, but without acquainting him with all the circumstances of the case, for I thought I was wise in being discreet.

I was exact to the appointed time, and Ismail received me with the utmost cordiality, but I was surprised when I found myself alone with him in the boat. We had two rowers and a man to steer; we took some fish, fried in oil, and ate it in the summer-house. The moon shone brightly, and the night was delightful. Alone with Ismail, and knowing his unnatural tastes, I did not feel very comfortable for, in spite of what M. de Bonneval had told me, I was afraid lest the Turk should take a fancy to give me too great a proof of his friendship, and I did not relish our tete-a-tete. But my fears were groundless.

"Let us leave this place quietly," said Ismail, "I have just heard a slight noise which heralds something that will amuse us."

He dismissed his attendants, and took my hand, saying,

"Let us go to a small room, the key of which I luckily have with me, but let us be careful not to make any noise. That room has a window overlooking the fountain where I think that two or three of my beauties have just gone to bathe. We will see them and enjoy a very pleasing sight, for they do not imagine that anyone is looking at them. They know that the place is forbidden to everybody except me."

We entered the room, we went to the window, and, the moon shining right over the basin of the fountain, we saw three nymphs who, now swimming, now standing or sitting on the marble steps, offered themselves to our eyes in every possible position, and in all the attitudes of graceful voluptuousness. Dear reader, I must not paint in too vivid colours the details of that beautiful picture, but if nature has endowed you with an ardent imagination and with equally ardent senses, you will easily imagine the fearful havoc which that unique, wonderful, and enchanting sight must have made upon my poor body.

A few days after that delightful fishing and bathing party by moonlight, I called upon Yusuf early in the morning; as it was raining, I could not go to the garden, and I went into the dining-room, in which I had never seen anyone. The moment I entered the room, a charming female form rose, covering her features with a thick veil which fell to the feet. A slave was sitting near the window, doing some tambour-work, but she did not move. I apologized, and turned to leave the room, but the lady stopped me, observing, with a sweet voice, that Yusuf had commanded her to entertain me before going out. She invited me to be seated, pointing to a rich cushion placed upon two larger ones, and I obeyed, while, crossing her legs, she sat down upon another cushion opposite to me. I thought I was looking upon Zelmi, and fancied that Yusuf had made up his mind to shew me that he was not less courageous than Ismail. Yet I was surprised, for, by such a proceeding, he strongly contradicted his maxims, and ran the risk of impairing the unbiased purity of my consent by throwing love in the balance. But I had no fear of that, because, to become enamoured, I should have required to see her face.

"I suppose," said the veiled beauty, "that you do not know who I am?"

"I could not guess, if I tried."

"I have been for the last five years the wife of your friend, and I am a native of Scio. I was thirteen years of age when I became his wife."

I was greatly astonished to find that my Mussulman philosopher had gone so far as to allow me to converse with his wife, but I felt more at ease after I had received that information, and fancied that I might carry the adventure further, but it would be necessary to see the lady's face, for a finely-dressed body, the head of which is not seen, excites but feeble desires. The fire lighted by amorous desires is like a fire of straw; the moment it burns up it is near its end. I had before me a magnificent appearance, but I could not see the soul of the image, for a thick gauze concealed it from my hungry gaze. I could see arms as white as alabaster, and hands like those of Alcina, 'dove ne nodo appalisce ne vena accede', and my active imagination fancied that all the rest was in harmony with those beautiful specimens, for the graceful folds of the muslin, leaving the outline all its perfection, hid from me only the living satin of the surface; there was no doubt that everything was lovely, but I wanted to see, in the expression of her eyes, that all that my imagination created had life and was endowed with feeling. The Oriental costume is a beautiful varnish placed upon a porcelain vase to protect from the touch the colours of the flowers and of the design, without lessening the pleasure of the eyes. Yusuf's wife was not dressed like a sultana; she wore the costume of Scio, with a short skirt which concealed neither the perfection of the leg nor the round form of the thigh, nor the voluptuous plump fall of the hips, nor the slender, well-made waist encompassed in a splendid band embroidered in silver and covered with arabesques. Above all those beauties, I could see the shape of two globes which Apelles would have taken for the model of those of his lovely Venus, and the rapid, inequal movement of which proved to me that those ravishing hillocks were animated. The small valley left between them, and which my eyes greedily feasted upon, seemed to me a lake of nectar, in which my burning lips longed to quench their thirst with more ardour than they would have drunk from the cup of the gods.

Enraptured, unable to control myself, I thrust my arm forward by a movement almost independent of my will, and my hand, too audacious, was on the point of lifting the hateful veil, but she prevented me by raising herself quickly on tiptoe, upbraiding me at the same time for my perfidious boldness, with a voice as commanding as her attitude.

"Dost thou deserve," she said, "Yusuf's friendship, when thou abusest the sacred laws of hospitality by insulting his wife?"

"Madam, you must kindly forgive me, for I never had any intention to insult you. In my country the lowest of men may fix his eyes upon the face of a queen."

"Yes, but he cannot tear off her veil, if she chooses to wear it. Yusuf shall avenge me."

The threat, and the tone in which it was pronounced, frightened me. I threw myself at her feet, and succeeded in calming her anger.

"Take a seat," she said.

And she sat down herself, crossing her legs with so much freedom that I caught a glimpse of charms which would have caused me to lose all control over myself if the delightful sight had remained one moment longer exposed to my eyes. I then saw that I had gone the wrong way to work, and I felt vexed with myself; but it was too late.

"Art thou excited?" she said.

"How could I be otherwise," I answered, "when thou art scorching me with an ardent fire?"

I had become more prudent, and I seized her hand without thinking any more of her face.

"Here is my husband," she said, and Yusuf came into the room. We rose, Yusuf embraced me, I complimented him, the slave left the room. Yusuf thanked his wife for having entertained me, and offered her his arm to take her to her own apartment. She took it, but when she reached the door, she raised her veil, and kissing her husband she allowed me to see her lovely face as if it had been done unwittingly. I followed her with my eyes as long as I could, and Yusuf, coming back to me, said with a laugh that his wife had offered to dine with us.

"I thought," I said to him, "that I had Zelmi before me."

"That would have been too much against our established rules. What I have done is not much, but I do not know an honest man who would be bold enough to bring his daughter into the presence of a stranger."

"I think your wife must be handsome; is she more beautiful than Zelmi?"

"My daughter's beauty is cheerful, sweet, and gentle; that of Sophia is proud and haughty. She will be happy after my death. The man who will marry her will find her a virgin."

I gave an account of my adventure to M. de Bonneval, somewhat exaggerating the danger I had run in trying to raise the veil of the handsome daughter of Scio.

"She was laughing at you," said the count, "and you ran no danger. She felt very sorry, believe me, to have to deal with a novice like you. You have been playing the comedy in the French fashion, when you ought to have gone straight to the point. What on earth did you want to see her nose for? She knew very well that she would have gained nothing by allowing you to see her. You ought to have secured the essential point. If I were young I would perhaps manage to give her a revenge, and to punish my friend Yusuf. You have given that lovely woman a poor opinion of Italian valour. The most reserved of Turkish women has no modesty except on her face, and, with her veil over it, she knows to a certainty that she will not blush at anything. I am certain that your beauty keeps her face covered whenever our friend Yusuf wishes to joke with her."

"She is yet a virgin."

"Rather a difficult thing to admit, my good friend; but I know the daughters of Scio; they have a talent for counterfeiting virginity."

Yusuf never paid me a similar compliment again, and he was quite right.

A few days after, I happened to be in the shop of an Armenian merchant, looking at some beautiful goods, when Yusuf entered the shop and praised my taste; but, although I had admired a great many things, I did not buy, because I thought they were too dear. I said so to Yusuf, but he remarked that they were, on the contrary, very cheap, and he purchased them all. We parted company at the door, and the next morning I received all the beautiful things he had bought; it was a delicate attention of my friend, and to prevent my refusal of such a splendid present, he had enclosed a note stating that, on my arrival in Corfu, he would let me know to whom the goods were to be delivered. He had thus sent me gold and silver filigrees from Damascus, portfolios, scarfs, belts, handkerchiefs and pipes, the whole worth four or five hundred piasters. When I called to thank him, I compelled him to confess that it was a present offered by his friendship.

The day before my departure from Constantinople, the excellent man burst into tears as I bade him adieu, and my grief was as great as his own. He told me that, by not accepting the offer of his daughter's hand, I had so strongly captivated his esteem that his feelings for me could not have been warmer if I had become his son. When I went on board ship with the Bailo Jean Dona, I found another case given to me by him, containing two quintals of the best Mocha coffee, one hundred pounds of tobacco leaves, two large flagons filled, one with Zabandi tobacco, the other with camussa, and a magnificent pipe tube of jessamine wood, covered with gold filigrane, which I sold in Corfu for one hundred sequins. I had not it in my power to give my generous Turk any mark of my gratitude until I reached Corfu, but there I did not fail to do so. I sold all his beautiful presents, which made me the possessor of a small fortune.

Ismail gave me a letter for the Chevalier de Lezze, but I could not forward it to him because I unfortunately lost it; he presented me with a barrel of hydromel, which I turned likewise into money. M. de Bonneval gave me a letter for Cardinal Acquaviva, which I sent to

Rome with an account of my journey, but his eminence did not think fit to acknowledge the receipt of either. Bonneval made me a present of twelve bottles of malmsey from Ragusa, and of twelve bottles of genuine scopolo—a great rarity, with which I made a present in Corfu which proved very useful to me, as the reader will discover.

The only foreign minister I saw much in Constantinople was the lord marshal of Scotland, the celebrated Keith, who represented the King of Prussia, and who, six years later was of great service to me in Paris.

We sailed from Constantinople in the beginning of September in the same man-of-war which had brought us, and we reached Corfu in fourteen days. The Bailo Dona did not land. He had with him eight splendid Turkish horses; I saw two of them still alive in Gorizia in the year 1773.

As soon as I had landed with my luggage, and had engaged a rather mean lodging, I presented myself to M. Andre Dolfin, the proveditore-generale, who promised me again that I should soon be promoted to a lieutenancy. After my visit to him, I called upon M. Camporese, my captain, and was well received by him. My third visit was to the commander of galleases, M. D—— R——, to whom M. Antonio Dolfin, with whom I had travelled from Venice to Corfu, had kindly recommended me. After a short conversation, he asked me if I would remain with him with the title of adjutant. I did not hesitate one instant, but accepted, saying how deeply honoured I felt by his offer, and assuring him that he would always find me ready to carry out his orders. He immediately had me taken to my room, and, the next day, I found myself established in his house. I obtained from my captain a French soldier to serve me, and I was well pleased when I found that the man was a hairdresser by trade, and a great talker by nature, for he could take care of my beautiful head of hair, and I wanted to practise French conversation. He was a good-for-nothing fellow, a drunkard and a debauchee, a peasant from Picardy, and he could hardly read or write, but I did not mind all that; all I wanted from him was to serve me, and to talk to me, and his French was pretty good. He was an amusing rogue, knowing by heart a quantity of erotic songs and of smutty stories which he could tell in the most laughable manner.

When I had sold my stock of goods from Constantinople (except the wines), I found myself the owner of nearly five hundred sequins. I redeemed all the articles which I had pledged in the hands of Jews, and turned into money everything of which I had no need. I was determined not to play any longer as a dupe, but to secure in gambling all the advantages which a prudent young man could obtain without sullying his honour.

I must now make my readers acquainted with the sort of life we were at that time leading in Corfu. As to the city itself, I will not describe it, because there are already many descriptions better than the one I could offer in these pages.

We had then in Corfu the 'proveditore-generale' who had sovereign authority, and lived in a style of great magnificence. That post was then filled by M. Andre Dolfin, a man sixty years of age, strict, headstrong, and ignorant. He no longer cared for women, but liked to be courted by them. He received every evening, and the supper-table was always laid for twenty-four persons.

We had three field-officers of the marines who did duty on the galleys, and three field-officers for the troops of the line on board the men-of-war. Each galeass had a captain called 'sopracomito', and we had ten of those captains; we had likewise ten commanders, one for each man-of-war, including three 'capi di mare', or admirals. They all belonged to the nobility of Venice. Ten young Venetian noblemen, from twenty to twenty-two years of age, were at Corfu as midshipmen in the navy. We had, besides, about a dozen civil clerks in the police of the island, or in the administration of justice, entitled 'grandi offciali di terra'. Those who were blessed with handsome wives had the pleasure of seeing their houses very much frequented by admirers who aspired to win the favours of the ladies, but there was not much heroic love-making, perhaps for the reason that there were then in Corfu many Aspasias whose favours could be had for money. Gambling was allowed everywhere, and that all absorbing passion was very prejudicial to the emotions of the heart.

The lady who was then most eminent for beauty and gallantry was Madame F——. Her husband, captain of a galley, had come to Corfu with her the year before, and madam had greatly astonished all the naval officers. Thinking that she had the privilege of the choice, she had given the preference to M. D——R——, and had dismissed all the suitors who presented themselves. M. F—— had married her on the very day she had left the convent; she was only seventeen years of age then, and he had brought her on board his galley immediately after the marriage ceremony.

I saw her for the first time at the dinner-table on the very day of my installation at M. D—— R——'s, and she made a great impression upon me. I thought I was gazing at a supernatural being, so infinitely above all the women I had ever seen, that it seemed impossible to fall in love with her She appeared to me of a nature different and so greatly superior to mine that I did not see the possibility of rising up to her. I even went so far as to persuade myself that nothing but a Platonic friendship could exist between her and M. D—— R——, and that M. F—— was quite right now not to shew any jealousy. Yet, that M. F—— was a perfect fool, and certainly not worthy of such a woman. The impression made upon me by Madame F—— was too ridiculous to last long, and the nature of it soon changed, but in a novel manner, at least as far as I was concerned.

My position as adjutant procured me the honour of dining at M. D—— R——'s table, but nothing more. The other adjutant, like me, an ensign in the army, but the greatest fool I had ever seen, shared that honour with me. We were not, however, considered as guests, for nobody ever spoke to us, and, what is more, no one ever honoured us with a look. It used to put me in a rage. I knew very well that people acted in that manner through no real contempt for us, but it went very hard with me. I could very well understand that my colleague, Sanzonio, should not complain of such treatment, because he was a blockhead, but I did not feel disposed to allow myself to be put on a par with him. At the end of eight or ten days, Madame F——, not having con descended to cast one glance upon my person, began to appear disagreeable to me. I felt piqued, vexed, provoked, and the more so because I could not suppose that the lady acted in that manner wilfully and purposely; I would have been highly pleased if there had been premeditation on her part. I felt satisfied that I was a nobody in her estimation, and as I was conscious of being somebody, I wanted her to know it. At last a circumstance offered itself in which, thinking that she could address me, she was compelled to look at me.

M. D—— R—— having observed that a very, very fine turkey had been placed before me, told me to carve it, and I immediately went to work. I was not a skilful carver, and Madame F——, laughing at my want of dexterity, told me that, if I had not been certain of performing my task with credit to myself, I ought not to have undertaken it. Full of confusion, and unable to answer her as my anger prompted, I sat down, with my heart overflowing with spite and hatred against her. To crown my rage, having one day to address me, she asked me what was my name. She had seen me every day for a fortnight, ever since I had been the adjutant of M. D—— R——; therefore she ought to have known my name. Besides, I had been very lucky at the gaming-table, and I had become rather famous in Corfu. My anger against Madame F was at its height.

I had placed my money in the hands of a certain Maroli, a major in the army and a gamester by profession, who held the faro bank at the coffee-house. We were partners; I helped him when he dealt, and he rendered me the same office when I held the cards, which was often the case, because he was not generally liked. He used to hold the cards in a way which frightened the punters; my manners were very different, and I was very lucky. Besides I was easy and smiling when my bank was losing, and I won without shewing any avidity, and that is a manner which always pleases the punters.

This Maroli was the man who had won all my money during my first stay in Corfu, and finding, when I returned, that I was resolved not to be duped any more, he judged me worthy of sharing the wise maxims without which gambling must necessarily ruin all those who meddle with it. But as Maroli had won my confidence only to a very slight extent, I was very careful. We made up our accounts every night, as soon as playing was over; the cashier kept the capital of the bank, the winnings were divided, and each took his share away. Lucky at play, enjoying good health and the friendship of my comrades, who, whenever the opportunity offered, always found me generous and ready to serve them, I would have been well pleased with my position if I had been a little more considered at the table of M. D—— R——, and treated with less haughtiness by his lady who, without any reason, seemed disposed to humiliate me. My self-love was deeply hurt, I hated her, and, with such a disposition of mind, the more I admired the perfection of her charms, the more I found her deficient in wit and intelligence. She might have made the conquest of my heart without bestowing hers upon me, for all I wanted was not to be compelled to hate her, and I could not understand what pleasure it could be for her to be detested, while with only a little kindness she could have been adored. I could not ascribe her manner to a spirit of coquetry, for I had never given her the slightest proof of the opinion I entertained of her beauty, and I could not therefore attribute her behaviour to a passion which might have rendered me disagreeable in her eyes; M. D—— R—— seemed to interest her only in a very slight manner, and as to her husband, she cared nothing for him. In short, that charming woman made me very unhappy, and I was angry with myself because I felt that, if it had not been for the manner in which she treated me, I would not have thought of her, and my vexation was increased by the feeling of hatred entertained by my heart against her, a feeling which until then I had never known to exist in me, and the discovery of which overwhelmed me with confusion.

One day a gentleman handed me, as we were leaving the dinner-table, a roll of gold that he had lost upon trust; Madame F—— saw it, and she said to me very abruptly,—

"What do you do with your money?"

"I keep it, madam, as a provision against possible losses."

"But as you do not indulge in any expense it would be better for you not to play; it is time wasted."

"Time given to pleasure is never time lost, madam; the only time which a young man wastes is that which is consumed in weariness, because when he is a prey to ennui he is likely to fall a prey to love, and to be despised by the object of his affection."

"Very likely; but you amuse yourself with hoarding up your money, and shew yourself to be a miser, and a miser is not less contemptible than a man in love. Why do you not buy yourself a pair of gloves?"

You may be sure that at these words the laughter was all on her side, and my vexation was all the greater because I could not deny that she was quite right. It was the adjutant's business to give the ladies an arm to their carriages, and it was not proper to fulfil that duty without gloves. I felt mortified, and the reproach of avarice hurt me deeply. I would a thousand times rather that she had laid my error to a want of education; and yet, so full of contradictions is the human heart, instead of making amends by adopting an appearance of elegance which the state of my finances enabled me to keep up, I did not purchase any gloves, and I resolved to avoid her and to abandon her to the insipid and dull gallantry of Sanzonio, who sported gloves, but whose teeth were rotten, whose breath was putrid, who wore a wig, and whose face seemed to be covered with shrivelled yellow parchment.

I spent my days in a continual state of rage and spite, and the most absurd part of it all was that I felt unhappy because I could not control my hatred for that woman whom, in good conscience, I could not find guilty of anything. She had for me neither love nor dislike, which was quite natural; but being young and disposed to enjoy myself I had become, without any wilful malice on her part, an eye-sore to her and the butt of her bantering jokes, which my sensitiveness exaggerated greatly. For all that I had an ardent wish to punish her and to make her repent. I thought of nothing else. At one time I would think of devoting all my intelligence and all my money to kindling an amorous passion in her heart, and then to revenge myself by treating her with contempt. But I soon realized the impracticability of such a plan, for even supposing that I should succeed in finding my way to her heart, was I the man to resist my own success with such a woman? I certainly could not flatter myself that I was so strong-minded. But I was the pet child of fortune, and my position was suddenly altered.

M. D—— R—— having sent me with dispatches to M. de Condulmer, captain of a 'galeazza', I had to wait until midnight to deliver them, and when I returned I found that M. D——R—— had retired to his apartment for the night. As soon as he was visible in the morning I went to him to render an account of my mission. I had been with him only a few minutes when his valet brought a letter saying that Madame F——'s adjutant was waiting for an answer. M. D——R—— read the note, tore it to pieces, and in his excitement stamped with his foot upon the fragments. He walked up and down the room for a little time, then wrote an answer and rang for the adjutant, to whom he delivered it. He then recovered his usual composure, concluded the perusal of the dispatch sent by M. de Condulmer, and told me to write a letter. He was looking it over when the valet came in, telling me that Madame F—— desired to see me. M. D——R—— told me that he did not require my services any more for the present, and that I might go. I left the room, but I had not gone ten yards when he called me back to remind me that my duty was to know nothing; I begged to assure him that I was well aware of that. I ran to Madame F——'s house, very eager to know what she wanted with me. I was introduced immediately, and I was greatly surprised to find her sitting up in bed, her countenance flushed and excited, and her eyes red from the tears she had evidently just been shedding. My heart was beating quickly, yet I did not know why.

"Pray be seated," she said, "I wish to speak with you."

"Madam," I answered, "I am not worthy of so great a favour, and I have not yet done anything to deserve it; allow me to remain standing."

She very likely recollected that she had never been so polite before, and dared not press me any further. She collected her thoughts for an instant or two, and said to me:

"Last evening my husband lost two hundred sequins upon trust at your faro bank; he believed that amount to be in my hands, and I must therefore give it to him immediately, as he is bound in honour to pay his losses to-day. Unfortunately I have disposed of the money, and I am in great trouble. I thought you might tell Maroli that I have paid you the amount lost by my husband. Here is a ring of some value; keep it until the 1st of January, when I will return the two hundred sequins for which I am ready to give you my note of hand."

"I accept the note of hand, madam, but I cannot consent to deprive you of your ring. I must also tell you that M. F—— must go himself to the bank, or send some one there, to redeem his debt. Within ten minutes you shall have the amount you require."

I left her without waiting for an answer, and I returned within a few minutes with the two hundred ducats, which I handed to her, and putting in my pocket her note of hand which she had just written, I bowed to take my leave, but she addressed to me these precious words:

"I believe, sir, that if I had known that you were so well disposed to oblige me, I could not have made up my mind to beg that service from you."

"Well, madam, for the future be quite certain that there is not a man in the world capable of refusing you such an insignificant service whenever you will condescend to ask for it in person."

"What you say is very complimentary, but I trust never to find myself again under the necessity of making such a cruel experiment."

I left Madame F——, thinking of the shrewdness of her answer. She had not told me that I was mistaken, as I had expected she would, for that would have caused her some humiliation: she knew that I was with M. D—— R—— when the adjutant had brought her letter, and she could not doubt that I was aware of the refusal she had met with. The fact of her not mentioning it proved to me that she was jealous of her own dignity; it afforded me great gratification, and I thought her worthy of adoration. I saw clearly that she could have no love for M. D—— R——, and that she was not loved by him, and the discovery made me leap for joy. From that moment I felt I was in love with her, and I conceived the hope that she might return my ardent affection.

The first thing I did, when I returned to my room, was to cross out with ink every word of her note of hand, except her name, in such a manner that it was impossible to guess at the contents, and putting it in an envelope carefully sealed, I deposited it in the hands of a public notary who stated, in the receipt he gave me of the envelope, that he would deliver it only to Madame F——, whenever she should request its delivery.

The same evening M. F—— came to the bank, paid me, played with cash in hand, and won some fifty ducats. What caused me the greatest surprise was that M. D—— R—— continued to be very gracious to Madame F——, and that she remained exactly the same towards him as she used to be before. He did not even enquire what she wanted when she had sent for me. But if she did not seem to change her manner towards my master, it was a very different case with me, for whenever she was opposite to me at dinner, she often addressed herself to me, and she thus gave me many opportunities of shewing my education and my wit in amusing stories or in remarks, in which I took care to blend instruction with witty jests. At that time F—— had the great talent of making others laugh while I kept a serious countenance myself. I had learnt that accomplishment from M. de Malipiero, my first master in the art of good breeding, who used to say to me,—

"If you wish your audience to cry, you must shed tears yourself, but if you wish to make them laugh you must contrive to look as serious as a judge."

In everything I did, in every word I uttered, in the presence of Madame F——, the only aim I had was to please her, but I did not wish her to suppose so, and I never looked at her unless she spoke to me. I wanted to force her curiosity, to compel her to suspect nay, to guess my secret, but without giving her any advantage over me: it was necessary for me to proceed by slow degrees. In the mean time, and until I should have a greater happiness, I was glad to see that my money, that magic talisman, and my good conduct, obtained me a consideration much greater than I could have hoped to obtain either through my position, or from my age, or in consequence of any talent I might have shewn in the profession I had adopted.

Towards the middle of November, the soldier who acted as my servant was attacked with inflammation of the chest; I gave notice of it to the captain of his company, and he was carried to the hospital. On the fourth day I was told that he would not recover, and that he had received the last sacraments; in the evening I happened to be at his captain's when the priest who had attended him came to announce his death, and to deliver a small parcel which the dying man had entrusted to him to be given up to his captain only after his death. The parcel contained a brass seal engraved with ducal arms, a certificate of baptism, and a sheet of paper covered with writing in French. Captain Camporese, who only spoke Italian, begged me to translate the paper, the contents of which were as follows:

"My will is that this paper, which I have written and signed with my own hand, shall be delivered to my captain only after I have breathed my last: until then, my confessor shall not make any use of it, for I entrust it to his hands only under the seal of confession. I entreat my captain to have me buried in a vault from which my body can be exhumed in case the duke, my father, should request its exhumation. I entreat him likewise to forward my certificate of baptism, the seal with the armorial bearings of my family, and a legal certificate of my birth to the French ambassador in Venice, who will send the whole to the duke, my father, my rights of primogeniture belonging, after my demise, to the prince, my brother. In faith of which I have signed and sealed these presents: Francois VI. Charles Philippe Louis Foucaud, Prince de la Rochefoucault."

The certificate of baptism, delivered at St. Sulpice gave the same names, and the title of the father was Francois V. The name of the mother was Gabrielle du Plessis.

As I was concluding my translation I could not help bursting into loud laughter; but the foolish captain, who thought my mirth out of place, hurried out to render an account of the affair to the proveditore-generale, and I went to the coffee-house, not doubting for one moment that his excellency would laugh at the captain, and that the post-mortem buffoonery would greatly amuse the whole of Corfu.

I had known in Rome, at Cardinal Acquaviva's, the Abbe de Liancourt, great-grandson of Charles, whose sister, Gabrielle du Plessis, had been the wife of Francois V, but that dated from the beginning of the last century. I had made a copy from the records of the cardinal of the account of certain circumstances which the Abbe de Liancourt wanted to communicate to the court of Spain, and in which there were a great many particulars respecting the house of Du Plessis. I thought at the same time that the singular imposture of La Valeur (such was the name by which my soldier generally went) was absurd and without a motive, since it was to be known only after his death, and could not therefore prove of any advantage to him.

Half an hour afterwards, as I was opening a fresh pack of cards, the Adjutant Sanzonio came in, and told the important news in the most serious manner. He had just come from the office of the proveditore, where Captain Camporese had run in the utmost hurry to deposit in the hands of his excellency the seal and the papers of the deceased prince. His excellency had immediately issued his orders for the burial of the prince in a vault with all the honours due to his exalted rank. Another half hour passed, and M. Minolto, adjutant of the proveditore-generale, came to inform me that his excellency wanted to see me. I passed the cards to Major Maroli, and went to his excellency's house. I found him at supper with several ladies, three or four naval commanders, Madame F——, and M. D—— R——.

"So, your servant was a prince!" said the old general to me.

"Your excellency, I never would have suspected it, and even now that he is dead I do not believe it."

"Why? He is dead, but he was not insane. You have seen his armorial bearings, his certificate of baptism, as well as what he wrote with his own hand. When a man is so near death, he does not fancy practical jokes."

"If your excellency is satisfied of the truth of the story, my duty is to remain silent."

"The story cannot be anything but true, and your doubts surprise me."

"I doubt, monsignor, because I happen to have positive information respecting the families of La Rochefoucault and Du Plessis. Besides, I have seen too much of the man. He was not a madman, but he certainly was an extravagant jester. I have never seen him write, and he has told me himself a score of times that he had never learned."

"The paper he has written proves the contrary. His arms have the ducal bearings; but perhaps you are not aware that M. de la Rochefoucault is a duke and peer of the French realm?"

"I beg your eminence's pardon; I know all about it; I know even more, for I know that Francois VI married a daughter of the house of Vivonne."

"You know nothing."

When I heard this remark, as foolish as it was rude, I resolved on remaining silent, and it was with some pleasure that I observed the joy felt by all the male guests at what they thought an insult and a blow to my vanity. An officer remarked that the deceased was a fine man, a witty man, and had shewn wonderful cleverness in keeping up his assumed character so well that no one ever had the faintest suspicion of what he really was. A lady said that, if she had known him, she would have been certain to find him out. Another flatterer, belonging to that mean, contemptible race always to be found near the great and wealthy of the earth, assured us that the late prince had always shewn himself cheerful, amiable, obliging, devoid of haughtiness towards his comrades, and that he used to sing beautifully. "He was only twenty-five years of age," said Madame Sagredo, looking me full in the face, "and if he was endowed with all those qualities, you must have discovered them."

"I can only give you, madam, a true likeness of the man, such as I have seen him. Always gay, often even to folly, for he could throw a somersault beautifully; singing songs of a very erotic kind, full of stories and of popular tales of magic, miracles, and ghosts, and a thousand marvellous feats which common-sense refused to believe, and which, for that very reason, provoked the mirth of his hearers. His faults were that he was drunken, dirty, quarrelsome, dissolute, and somewhat of a cheat. I put up with all his deficiences, because he dressed my hair to my taste, and his constant chattering offered me the opportunity of practising the colloquial French which cannot be acquired from books. He has always assured me that he was born in Picardy, the son of a common peasant, and that he had deserted from the French army. He may have deceived me when he said that he could not write."

Just then Camporese rushed into the room, and announced that La Veleur was yet breathing. The general, looking at me significantly, said that he would be delighted if the man could be saved.

"And I likewise, monsignor, but his confessor will certainly kill him to-night."

"Why should the father confessor kill him?"

"To escape the galleys to which your excellency would not fail to send him for having violated the secrecy of the confessional."

Everybody burst out laughing, but the foolish old general knitted his brows. The guests retired soon afterwards, and Madame F——, whom I had preceded to the carriage, M. D—— R—— having offered her his arm, invited me to get in with her, saying that it was raining. It was the first time that she had bestowed such an honour upon me.

"I am of your opinion about that prince," she said, "but you have incurred the displeasure of the proveditore."

"I am very sorry, madam, but it could not have been avoided, for I cannot help speaking the truth openly."

"You might have spared him," remarked M. D—— R——, "the cutting jest of the confessor killing the false prince."

"You are right, sir, but I thought it would make him laugh as well as it made madam and your excellency. In conversation people generally do not object to a witty jest causing merriment and laughter."

"True; only those who have not wit enough to laugh do not like the jest."

"I bet a hundred sequins that the madman will recover, and that, having the general on his side, he will reap all the advantages of his imposture. I long to see him treated as a prince, and making love to Madame Sagredo."

Hearing the last words, Madame F——, who did not like Madame Sagredo, laughed heartily, and, as we were getting out of the carriage, M. D—— R—— invited me to accompany them upstairs. He was in the habit of spending half an hour alone with her at her own house when they had taken supper together with the general, for her husband never shewed himself. It was the first time that the happy couple admitted a third person to their tete-a-tete. I felt very proud of the compliment thus paid to me, and I thought it might have important results for me. My satisfaction, which I concealed as well as I could, did not prevent me from being very gay and from giving a comic turn to every subject brought forward by the lady or by her lord.

We kept up our pleasant trio for four hours; and returned to the mansion of M. D—— R—— only at two o'clock in the morning. It was during that night that Madame F—— and M. D—— R—— really made my acquaintance. Madame F—— told him that she had never laughed so much, and that she had never imagined that a conversation, in appearance so simple, could afford so much pleasure and merriment. On my side, I discovered in her so much wit and cheerfulness, that I became deeply enamoured, and went to bed fully satisfied that, in the future, I could not keep up the show of indifference which I had so far assumed towards her.

When I woke up the next morning, I heard from the new soldier who served me that La Valeur was better, and had been pronounced out of danger by the physician. At dinner the conversation fell upon him, but I did not open my lips. Two days afterwards, the general gave orders to have him removed to a comfortable apartment, sent him a servant, clothed him, and the over-credulous proveditore having paid him a visit, all the naval commanders and officers thought it their duty to imitate him, and to follow his example: the general curiosity was excited, there was a rush to see the new prince. M. D—— R——

followed his leaders, and Madame Sagredo, having set the ladies in motion, they all called upon him, with the exception of Madame F——, who told me laughingly that she would not pay him a visit unless I would consent to introduce her. I begged to be excused. The knave was called your highness, and the wonderful prince styled Madame Sagredo his princess. M. D—— R—— tried to persuade me to call upon the rogue, but I told him that I had said too much, and that I was neither courageous nor mean enough to retract my words. The whole imposture would soon have been discovered if anyone had possessed a peerage, but it just happened that there was not a copy in Corfu, and the French consul, a fat blockhead, like many other consuls, knew nothing of family trees. The madcap La Valeur began to walk out a week after his metamorphosis into a prince. He dined and had supper every day with the general, and every evening he was present at the reception, during which, owing to his intemperance, he always went fast asleep. Yet, there were two reasons which kept up the belief of his being a prince: the first was that he did not seem afraid of the news expected from Venice, where the proveditore had written immediately after the discovery; the second was that he solicited from the bishop the punishment of the priest who had betrayed his secret by violating the seal of confession. The poor priest had already been sent to prison, and the proveditore had not the courage to defend him. The new prince had been invited to dinner by all the naval officers, but M. D—— R—— had not made up his mind to imitate them so far, because Madame F—— had clearly warned him that she would dine at her own house on the day he was invited. I had likewise respectfully intimated that, on the same occasion, I would take the liberty of dining somewhere else.

I met the prince one day as I was coming out of the old fortress leading to the esplanade. He stopped, and reproached me for not having called upon him. I laughed, and advised him to think of his safety before the arrival of the news which would expose all the imposture, in which case the proveditore was certain to treat him very severely. I offered to help him in his flight from Corfu, and to get a Neapolitan captain, whose ship was ready to sail, to conceal him on board; but the fool, instead of accepting my offer, loaded me with insults.

He was courting Madame Sagredo, who treated him very well, feeling proud that a French prince should have given her the preference over all the other ladies. One day that she was dining in great ceremony at M. D——R——'s house, she asked me why I had advised the prince to run away.

"I have it from his own lips," she added, "and he cannot make out your obstinacy in believing him an impostor."

"I have given him that advice, madam, because my heart is good, and my judgment sane."

"Then we are all of us as many fools, the proveditore included?"

"That deduction would not be right, madam. An opinion contrary to that of another does not necessarily make a fool of the person who entertains it. It might possibly turn out, in ten or twelve days, that I have been entirely mistaken myself, but I should not consider myself a fool in consequence. In the mean time, a lady of your intelligence must have discovered whether that man is a peasant or a prince by his education and manners. For instance, does he dance well?"

"He does not know one step, but he is the first to laugh about it; he says he never would learn dancing."

"Does he behave well at table?"

"Well, he doesn't stand on ceremony. He does not want his plate to be changed, he helps himself with his spoon out of the dishes; he does not know how to check an eructation or a yawn, and if he feels tired he leaves the table. It is evident that he has been very badly brought up."

"And yet he is very pleasant, I suppose. Is he clean and neat?"

"No, but then he is not yet well provided with linen."

"I am told that he is very sober."

"You are joking. He leaves the table intoxicated twice a day, but he ought to be pitied, for he cannot drink wine and keep his head clear. Then he swears like a trooper, and we all laugh, but he never takes offence."

"Is he witty?"

"He has a wonderful memory, for he tells us new stories every day."

"Does he speak of his family?"

"Very often of his mother, whom he loved tenderly. She was a Du Plessis."

"If his mother is still alive she must be a hundred and fifty years old."

"What nonsense!"

"Not at all; she was married in the days of Marie de Medicis."

"But the certificate of baptism names the prince's mother, and his seal—"

"Does he know what armorial bearings he has on that seal?"

"Do you doubt it?"

"Very strongly, or rather I am certain that he knows nothing about it."

We left the table, and the prince was announced. He came in, and Madame Sagredo lost no time in saying to him, "Prince, here is M. Casanova; he pretends that you do not know your own armorial bearings." Hearing these words, he came up to me, sneering, called me a coward, and gave me a smack on the face which almost stunned me. I left the room very slowly, not forgetting my hat and my cane, and went downstairs, while M. D—— R—— was loudly ordering the servants to throw the madman out of the window.

I left the palace and went to the esplanade in order to wait for him. The moment I saw him, I ran to meet him, and I beat him so violently with my cane that one blow alone ought to have killed him. He drew back, and found himself brought to a stand between two walls, where, to avoid being beaten to death, his only resource was to draw his sword, but the cowardly scoundrel did not even think of his weapon, and I left him, on the ground, covered with blood. The crowd formed a line for me to pass, and I went to the coffee-house, where I drank a glass of lemonade, without sugar to precipitate the bitter saliva which rage had brought up from my stomach. In a few minutes, I found myself surrounded by all the young officers of the garrison, who joined in the general opinion that I ought to have killed him, and they at last annoyed me, for it was not my fault if I had not done so, and I would certainly have taken his life if he had drawn his sword.

I had been in the coffee-house for half an hour when the general's adjutant came to tell me that his excellency ordered me to put myself under arrest on board the bastarda, a galley on which the prisoners had their legs in irons like galley slaves. The dose was rather too strong to be swallowed, and I did not feel disposed to submit to it. "Very good, adjutant," I replied, "it shall be done." He went away, and I left the coffee-house a moment after him, but when I reached the end of the street, instead of going towards the esplanade, I proceeded quickly towards the sea. I walked along the beach for a quarter of an hour, and finding a boat empty, but with a pair of oars, I got in her, and unfastening her, I rowed as hard as I could towards a large caicco, sailing against the wind with six oars. As soon as I had come up to her, I went on board and asked the carabouchiri to sail before the wind and to take me to a large wherry which could be seen at some distance, going towards Vido Rock. I abandoned the row-boat, and, after paying the master of the caicco generously, I got into the wherry, made a bargain with the skipper who unfurled three sails, and in less than two hours we were fifteen miles away from Corfu. The wind having died away, I made the men row against the current, but towards midnight they told me that they could not row any longer, they were worn out with fatigue. They advised me to sleep until day-break, but I refused to do so, and for a trifle I got them to put me on shore, without asking where I was, in order not to raise their suspicions. It was enough for me to know that I was at a distance of twenty miles from Corfu, and in a place where nobody could imagine me to be. The moon was shining, and I saw a church with a house adjoining, a long barn opened on both sides, a plain of about one hundred yards confined by hills, and nothing more. I found some straw in the barn, and laying myself down, I slept until day-break in spite of the cold. It was the 1st of December, and although the climate is very mild in Corfu I felt benumbed when I awoke, as I had no cloak over my thin uniform.

The bells begin to toll, and I proceed towards the church. The long-bearded papa, surprised at my sudden apparition, enquires whether I am Romeo (a Greek); I tell him that I am Fragico (Italian), but he turns his back upon me and goes into his house, the door of which he shuts without condescending to listen to me.

I then turned towards the sea, and saw a boat leaving a tartan lying at anchor within one hundred yards of the island; the boat had four oars and landed her passengers. I come up to them and meet a good-looking Greek, a woman and a young boy ten or twelve years old. Addressing myself to the Greek, I ask him whether he has had a pleasant passage, and where he comes from. He answers in Italian that he has sailed from Cephalonia with his wife and his son, and that he is bound for Venice; he had landed to hear mass at the Church of Our Lady of Casopo, in order to ascertain whether his father-in-law was still alive, and whether he would pay the amount he had promised him for the dowry of his wife.

"But how can you find it out?"

"The Papa Deldimopulo will tell me; he will communicate faithfully the oracle of the Holy Virgin." I say nothing and follow him into the church; he speaks to the priest, and gives him some money. The papa says the mass, enters the sanctum sanctorum, comes out again in a quarter of an hour, ascends the steps of the altar, turns towards his audience, and, after meditating for a minute and stroking his long beard, he delivers his oracle in a dozen words. The Greek of Cephalonia, who certainly could not boast of being as wise as Ulysses, appears very well pleased, and gives more money to the impostor. We leave the church, and I ask him whether he feels satisfied with the oracle.

"Oh! quite satisfied. I know now that my father-in-law is alive, and that he will pay me the dowry, if I consent to leave my child with him. I am aware that it is his fancy and I will give him the boy."

"Does the papa know you?"

"No; he is not even acquainted with my name."

"Have you any fine goods on board your tartan?"

"Yes; come and breakfast with me; you can see all I have."

"Very willingly."

Delighted at hearing that oracles were not yet defunct, and satisfied that they will endure as long as there are in this world simple-minded men and deceitful, cunning priests, I follow the good man, who took me to his tartan and treated me to an excellent breakfast. His cargo consisted of cotton, linen, currants, oil, and excellent wines. He had also a stock of night-caps, stockings, cloaks in the Eastern fashion, umbrellas, and sea biscuits, of which I was very fond; in those days I had thirty teeth, and it would have been difficult to find a finer set. Alas! I have but two left now, the other twenty-eight are gone with other tools quite as precious; but 'dum vita super est, bene est.' I bought a small stock of everything he had except cotton, for which I had no use, and without discussing his price I paid him the thirty-five or forty sequins he demanded, and seeing my generosity he made me a present of six beautiful botargoes.

I happened during our conversation to praise the wine of Xante, which he called generoydes, and he told me that if I would accompany him to Venice he would give me a bottle of that wine every day including the quarantine. Always superstitious, I was on the point of accepting, and that for the most foolish reason-namely, that there would be no premeditation in that strange resolution, and it might be the impulse of fate. Such was my nature in those days; alas; it is very different now. They say that it is because wisdom comes with old age, but I cannot reconcile myself to cherish the effect of a most unpleasant cause.

Just as I was going to accept his offer he proposes to sell me a very fine gun for ten sequins, saying that in Corfu anyone would be glad of it for twelve. The word Corfu upsets all my ideas on the spot! I fancy I hear the voice of my genius telling me to go back to that city. I purchase the gun for the ten sequins, and my honest Cephalonian, admiring my fair dealing, gives me, over and above our bargain, a beautiful Turkish pouch well filled with powder and shot. Carrying my gun, with a good warm cloak over my uniform and with a large bag containing all my purchases, I take leave of the worthy Greek, and am landed on the shore, determined on obtaining a lodging from the cheating papa, by fair means or foul. The good wine of my friend the Cephalonian had excited me just enough to make me carry my determination into immediate execution. I had in my pockets four or five hundred copper gazzette, which were very heavy, but which I had procured from the Greek, foreseeing that I might want them during my stay on the island.

I store my bag away in the barn and I proceed, gun in hand, towards the house of the priest; the church was closed.

I must give my readers some idea of the state I was in at that moment. I was quietly hopeless. The three or four hundred sequins I had with me did not prevent me from thinking that I was not in very great security on the island; I could not remain long, I would soon be found out, and, being guilty of desertion, I should be treated accordingly. I did not know what to do, and that is always an unpleasant predicament. It would be absurd for me to return to Corfu of my own accord; my flight would then be useless, and I should be thought a fool, for my return would be a proof of cowardice or stupidity; yet I did not feel the courage to desert altogether. The chief cause of my decision was not that I had a thousand sequins in the hands of the faro banker, or my well-stocked wardrobe, or the fear of not getting a living somewhere else, but the unpleasant recollection that I should leave behind me a woman whom I loved to adoration, and from whom I had not yet obtained any favour, not even that of kissing her hand. In such distress of mind I could not do anything else but abandon myself to chance, whatever the result might be, and the most essential thing for the present was to secure a lodging and my daily food.

I knock at the door of the priest's dwelling. He looks out of a window and shuts it without listening to me, I knock again, I swear, I call out loudly, all in vain, Giving way to my rage, I take aim at a poor sheep grazing with several others at a short distance, and kill it. The herdsman begins to scream, the papa shows himself at the window, calling out, "Thieves! Murder!" and orders the alarm-bell to be rung. Three bells are immediately set in motion, I foresee a general gathering: what is going to happen? I do not know, but happen what will, I load my gun and await coming events.

In less than eight or ten minutes, I see a crowd of peasants coming down the hills, armed with guns, pitchforks, or cudgels: I withdraw inside of the barn, but without the slightest fear, for I cannot suppose that, seeing me alone, these men will murder me without listening to me.

The first ten or twelve peasants come forward, gun in hand and ready to fire: I stop them by throwing down my gazzette, which they lose no time in picking up from the ground, and I keep on throwing money down as the men come forward, until I had no more left. The clowns were looking at each other in great astonishment, not knowing what to make out of a well-dressed young man, looking very peaceful, and throwing his money to them with such generosity. I could not speak to them until the deafening noise of the bells should cease. I quietly sit down on my large bag, and keep still, but as soon as I can be heard I begin to address the men. The priest, however, assisted by his beadle and by the herdsman, interrupts me, and all the more easily that I was speaking Italian. My three enemies, who talked all at once, were trying to excite the crowd against me.

One of the peasants, an elderly and reasonable-looking man, comes up to me and asks me in Italian why I have killed the sheep.

"To eat it, my good fellow, but not before I have paid for it."

"But his holiness, the papa, might choose to charge one sequin for it."

"Here is one sequin."

The priest takes the money and goes away: war is over. The peasant tells me that he has served in the campaign of 1716, and that he was at the defence of Corfu. I compliment him, and ask him to find me a lodging and a man able to prepare my meals. He answers that he will procure me a whole house, that he will be my cook himself, but I must go up the hill. No matter! He calls two stout fellows, one takes my bag, the other shoulders my sheep, and forward! As we are walking along, I tell him,—

"My good man, I would like to have in my service twenty-four fellows like these under military discipline. I would give each man twenty gazzette a day, and you would have forty as my lieutenant."

"I will," says the old soldier, "raise for you this very day a body-guard of which you will be proud."

We reach a very convenient house, containing on the ground floor three rooms and a stable, which I immediately turned into a guard-room.

My lieutenant went to get what I wanted, and particularly a needlewoman to make me some shirts. In the course of the day I had furniture, bedding, kitchen utensils, a good dinner, twenty-four well-equipped soldiers, a super-annuated sempstress and several young girls to make my shirts. After supper, I found my position highly pleasant, being surrounded with some thirty persons who looked upon me as their sovereign, although they could not make out what had brought me to their island. The only thing which struck me as disagreeable was that the young girls could not speak Italian, and I did not know Greek enough to enable me to make love to them.

The next morning my lieutenant had the guard relieved, and I could not help bursting into a merry laugh. They were like a flock of sheep: all fine men, well-made and strong; but without uniform and without discipline the finest band is but a herd. However, they quickly learned how to present arms and to obey the orders of their officer. I caused three sentinels to be placed, one before the guardroom, one at my door, and the third where he could have a good view of the sea. This sentinel was to give me warning of the approach of any armed boat or vessel. For the first two or three days I considered all this as mere amusement, but, thinking that I might really want the men to repel force by force, I had some idea of making my army take an oath of allegiance. I did not do so, however, although my lieutenant assured me that I had only to express my wishes, for my generosity had captivated the love of all the islanders.

My sempstress, who had procured some young needlewomen to sew my shirts, had expected that I would fall in love with one and not with all, but my amorous zeal overstepped her hopes, and all the pretty ones had their turn; they were all well satisfied with me, and the sempstress was rewarded for her good offices. I was leading a delightful life, for my table was supplied with excellent dishes, juicy mutton, and snipe so delicious that I have never tasted their like except in St. Petersburg. I drank scopolo wine or the best muscatel of the Archipelago. My lieutenant was my only table companion. I never took a walk without him and two of my body-guard, in order to defend myself against the attacks of a few young men who had a spite against me because they fancied, not without some reason, that my needlewomen, their mistresses, had left them on my account. I often thought while I was rambling about the island, that without money I should have been unhappy, and that I was indebted to my gold for all the happiness I was enjoying; but it was right to suppose at the same time that, if I had not felt my purse pretty heavy, I would not have been likely to leave Corfu.

I had thus been playing the petty king with success for a week or ten days, when, towards ten o'clock at night I heard the sentinel's challenge. My lieutenant went out, and returned announcing that an honest-looking man, who spoke Italian, wished to see me on important business. I had him brought in, and, in the presence of my lieutenant, he told me in Italian:

"Next Sunday, the Papa Deldimopulo will fulminate against you the 'cataramonachia'. If you do not prevent him, a slow fever will send you into the next world in six weeks."

"I have never heard of such a drug."

"It is not a drug. It is a curse pronounced by a priest with the Host in his hands, and it is sure to be fulfilled."

"What reason can that priest have to murder me?"

"You disturb the peace and discipline of his parish. You have seduced several young girls, and now their lovers refuse to marry them."

I made him drink, and thanking him heartily, wished him good night. His warning struck me as deserving my attention, for, if I had no fear of the 'cataramonachia', in which I had not the slightest faith, I feared certain poisons which might be by far more efficient. I passed a very quiet night, but at day-break I got up, and without saying anything to my lieutenant, I went straight to the church where I found the priest, and addressed him in the following words, uttered in a tone likely to enforce conviction:

"On the first symptom of fever, I will shoot you like a dog. Throw over me a curse which will kill me instantly, or make your will. Farewell!"

Having thus warned him, I returned to my royal palace. Early on the following Monday, the papa called on me. I had a slight headache; he enquired after my health, and when I told him that my head felt rather heavy, he made me laugh by the air of anxiety with which he assured me that it could be caused by nothing else than the heavy atmosphere of the island of Casopo.

Three days after his visit, the advanced sentinel gave the war-cry. The lieutenant went out to reconnoitre, and after a short absence he gave me notice that the long boat of an armed vessel had just landed an officer. Danger was at hand.

I go out myself, I call my men to arms, and, advancing a few steps, I see an officer, accompanied by a guide, who was walking towards my dwelling. As he was alone, I had nothing to fear. I return to my room, giving orders to my lieutenant to receive him with all military honours and to introduce him. Then, girding my sword, I wait for my visitor.

In a few minutes, Adjutant Minolto, the same who had brought me the order to put myself under arrest, makes his appearance.

"You are alone," I say to him, "and therefore you come as a friend. Let us embrace."

"I must come as a friend, for, as an enemy, I should not have enough men. But what I see seems a dream."

"Take a seat, and dine with me. I will treat you splendidly."

"Most willingly, and after dinner we will leave the island together."

"You may go alone, if you like; but I will not leave this place until I have the certainty, not only that I shall not be sent to the 'bastarda', but also that I shall have every satisfaction from the knave whom the general ought to send to the galleys."

"Be reasonable, and come with me of your own accord. My orders are to take you by force, but as I have not enough men to do so, I shall make my report, and the general will, of course, send a force sufficient to arrest you."

"Never; I will not be taken alive."

"You must be mad; believe me, you are in the wrong. You have disobeyed the order I brought you to go to the 'bastarda; in that you have acted wrongly, and in that alone, for in every other respect you were perfectly right, the general himself says so."

"Then I ought to have put myself under arrest?"

"Certainly; obedience is necessary in our profession."

"Would you have obeyed, if you had been in my place?"

"I cannot and will not tell you what I would have done, but I know that if I had disobeyed orders I should have been guilty of a crime."

"But if I surrendered now I should be treated like a criminal, and much more severely than if I had obeyed that unjust order."

"I think not. Come with me, and you will know everything."

"What! Go without knowing what fate may be in store for me? Do not expect it. Let us have dinner. If I am guilty of such a dreadful crime that violence must be used against me, I will surrender only to irresistible force. I cannot be worse off, but there may be blood spilled."

"You are mistaken, such conduct would only make you more guilty. But I say like you, let us have dinner. A good meal will very likely render you more disposed to listen to reason."

Our dinner was nearly over, when we heard some noise outside. The lieutenant came in, and informed me that the peasants were gathering in the neighbourhood of my house to defend me, because a rumour had spread through the island that the felucca had been sent with orders to arrest me and take me to Corfu. I told him to undeceive the good fellows, and to send them away, but to give them first a barrel of wine.

The peasants went away satisfied, but, to shew their devotion to me, they all fired their guns.

"It is all very amusing," said the adjutant, "but it will turn out very serious if you let me go away alone, for my duty compels me to give an exact account of all I have witnessed."

"I will follow you, if you will give me your word of honour to land me free in Corfu."

"I have orders to deliver your person to M. Foscari, on board the bastarda."

"Well, you shall not execute your orders this time."

"If you do not obey the commands of the general, his honour will compel him to use violence against you, and of course he can do it. But tell me, what would you do if the general should leave you in this island for the sake of the joke? There is no fear of that, however, and, after the report which I must give, the general will certainly make up his mind to stop the affair without shedding blood."

"Without a fight it will be difficult to arrest me, for with five hundred peasants in such a place as this I would not be afraid of three thousand men."

"One man will prove enough; you will be treated as a leader of rebels. All these peasants may be devoted to you, but they cannot protect you against one man who will shoot you for the sake of earning a few pieces of gold. I can tell you more than that: amongst all those men who surround you there is not one who would not murder you for twenty sequins. Believe me, go with me. Come to enjoy the triumph which is awaiting you in Corfu. You will be courted and applauded. You will narrate yourself all your mad frolics, people will laugh, and at the same time will admire you for having listened to reason the moment I came here. Everybody feels esteem for you, and M. D—— R—— thinks a great deal of you. He praises very highly the command you have shewn over your passion in refraining from thrusting your sword through that insolent fool, in order not to forget the respect you owed to his house.

The general himself must esteem you, for he cannot forget what you told him of that knave."

"What has become of him?"

"Four days ago Major Sardina's frigate arrived with dispatches, in which the general must have found all the proof of the imposture, for he has caused the false duke or prince to disappear very suddenly. Nobody knows where he has been sent to, and nobody ventures to mention the fellow before the general, for he made the most egregious blunder respecting him."

"But was the man received in society after the thrashing I gave him?"

"God forbid! Do you not recollect that he wore a sword? From that moment no one would receive him. His arm was broken and his jaw shattered to pieces.

"But in spite of the state he was in, in spite of what he must have suffered, his excellency had him removed a week after you had treated him so severely. But your flight is what everyone has been wondering over. It was thought for three days that M. D——R——had concealed you in his house, and he was openly blamed for doing so. He had to declare loudly at the general's table that he was in the most complete ignorance of your whereabouts. His excellency even expressed his anxiety about your escape, and it was only yesterday that your place of refuge was made known by a letter addressed by the priest of this island to the Proto-Papa Bulgari, in which he complained that an Italian officer had invaded the island of Casopo a week before, and had committed unheard-of violence. He accused you of seducing all the girls, and of threatening to shoot him if he dared to pronounce 'cataramonachia' against you. This letter, which was read publicly at the evening reception, made the general laugh, but he ordered me to arrest you all the same."

"Madame Sagredo is the cause of it all."

"True, but she is well punished for it. You ought to call upon her with me to-morrow."

"To-morrow? Are you then certain that I shall not be placed under arrest?"

"Yes, for I know that the general is a man of honour."

"I am of the same opinion. Well, let us go on board your felucca. We will embark together after midnight."

"Why not now?"

"Because I will not run the risk of spending the night on board M. Foscari's bastarda. I want to reach Corfu by daylight, so as to make your victory more brilliant."

"But what shall we do for the next eight hours?"

"We will pay a visit to some beauties of a species unknown in Corfu, and have a good supper."

I ordered my lieutenant to send plenty to eat and to drink to the men on board the felucca, to prepare a splendid supper, and to spare nothing, as I should leave the island at midnight. I made him a present of all my provisions, except such as I wanted to take with me; these I sent on board. My janissaries, to whom I gave a week's pay, insisted upon escorting me, fully equipped, as far as the boat, which made the adjutant laugh all the way.

We reached Corfu by eight o'clock in the morning, and we went alongside the 'bastarda. The adjutant consigned me to M. Foscari, assuring me that he would immediately give notice of my arrival to M. D——R——, send my luggage to his house, and report the success of his expedition to the general.

M. Foscari, the commander of the bastarda, treated me very badly. If he had been blessed with any delicacy of feeling, he would not have been in such a hurry to have me put in irons. He might have talked to me, and have thus delayed for a quarter of an hour that operation which greatly vexed me. But, without uttering a single word, he sent me to the 'capo di scalo' who made me sit down, and told me to put my foot forward to receive the irons, which, however, do not dishonour anyone in that country, not even the galley slaves, for they are better treated than soldiers.

My right leg was already in irons, and the left one was in the hands of the man for the completion of that unpleasant ceremony, when the adjutant of his excellency came to tell the executioner to set me at liberty and to return me my sword. I wanted to present my compliments to the noble M. Foscari, but the adjutant, rather ashamed, assured me that his excellency did not expect me to do so. The first thing I did was to pay my respects to the general, without saying one word to him, but he told me with a serious countenance to be more prudent for the future, and to learn that a soldier's first duty was to obey, and above all to be modest and discreet. I understood perfectly the meaning of the two last words, and acted accordingly.

When I made my appearance at M. D——R——'s, I could see pleasure on everybody's face. Those moments have always been so dear to me that I have never forgotten them, they have afforded me consolation in the time of adversity. If you would relish pleasure you must endure pain, and delights are in proportion to the privations we have suffered. M. D—— R—— was so glad to see me that he came up to me and warmly embraced me. He presented me with a beautiful ring which he took from his own finger, and told me that I had acted quite rightly in not letting anyone, and particularly himself, know where I had taken refuge.

"You can't think," he added, frankly, "how interested Madame F—— was in your fate. She would be really delighted if you called on her immediately."

How delightful to receive such advice from his own lips! But the word "immediately" annoyed me, because, having passed the night on board the felucca, I was afraid that the disorder of my toilet might injure me in her eyes. Yet I could neither refuse M. D—— R——, nor tell him the reason of my refusal, and I bethought myself that I could make a merit of it in the eyes of Madame F—— I therefore went at once to her house; the goddess was not yet visible, but her attendant told me to come in, assuring me that her mistress's bell would soon be heard, and that she would be very sorry if I did not wait to see her. I spent half an hour with that young and indiscreet person, who was a very charming girl, and learned from her many things which caused me great pleasure, and particularly all that had been said respecting my escape. I found that throughout the affair my conduct had met with general approbation.

As soon as Madame F—— had seen her maid, she desired me to be shewn in. The curtains were drawn aside, and I thought I saw Aurora surrounded with the roses and the pearls of morning. I told her that, if it had not been for the order I received from M. D—— R—— I would not have presumed to present myself before her in my travelling costume; and in the most friendly tone she answered that M. D—— R——, knowing all the interest she felt in me, had been quite right to tell me to come, and she assured me that M. D—— R—— had the greatest esteem for me.

"I do not know, madam, how I have deserved such great happiness, for all I dared aim at was toleration."

"We all admired the control you kept over your feelings when you refrained from killing that insolent madman on the spot; he would have been thrown out of the window if he had not beat a hurried retreat."

"I should certainly have killed him, madam, if you had not been present."

"A very pretty compliment, but I can hardly believe that you thought of me in such a moment."

I did not answer, but cast my eyes down, and gave a deep sigh. She observed my new ring, and in order to change the subject of conversation she praised M. D—— R—— very highly, as soon as I had told her how he had offered it to me. She desired me to give her an account of my life on the island, and I did so, but allowed my pretty needlewomen to remain under a veil, for I had already learnt that in this world the truth must often remain untold.

All my adventures amused her much, and she greatly admired my conduct.

"Would you have the courage," she said, "to repeat all you have just told me, and exactly in the same terms, before the proveditore-generale?"

"Most certainly, madam, provided he asked me himself."

"Well, then, prepare to redeem your promise. I want our excellent general to love you and to become your warmest protector, so as to shield you against every injustice and to promote your advancement. Leave it all to me."

Her reception fairly overwhelmed me with happiness, and on leaving her house I went to Major Maroli to find out the state of my finances. I was glad to hear that after my escape he had no longer considered me a partner in the faro bank. I took four hundred sequins from the cashier, reserving the right to become again a partner, should circumstances prove at any time favourable.

In the evening I made a careful toilet, and called for the Adjutant Minolto in order to pay with him a visit to Madame Sagredo, the general's favourite. With the exception of Madame F—— she was the greatest beauty of Corfu. My visit surprised her, because, as she had been the cause of all that had happened, she was very far from expecting it. She imagined that I had a spite against her. I undeceived her, speaking to her very candidly, and she treated me most kindly, inviting me to come now and then to spend the evening at her house.

But I neither accepted nor refused her amiable invitation, knowing that Madame F—— disliked her; and how could I be a frequent guest at her house with such a knowledge! Besides, Madame Sagredo was very fond of gambling, and, to please her, it was necessary either to lose or make her win, but to accept such conditions one must be in love with the lady or wish to make her conquest, and I had not the slightest idea of either. The Adjutant Minolto never played, but he had captivated the lady's good graces by his services in the character of Mercury.

When I returned to the palace I found Madame F—— alone, M. D—— R—— being engaged with his correspondence. She asked me to sit near her, and to tell her all my adventures in Constantinople. I did so, and I had no occasion to repent it. My meeting with Yusuf's wife pleased her extremely, but the bathing scene by moonlight made her blush with excitement. I veiled as much as I could the too brilliant colours of my picture, but, if she did not find me clear, she would oblige me to be more explicit, and if I made myself better understood by giving to my recital a touch of voluptuousness which I borrowed from her looks more than from my recollection, she would scold me and tell me that I might have disguised a little more. I felt that the way she was talking would give her a liking for me, and I was satisfied that the man who can give birth to amorous desires is easily called upon to gratify them it was the reward I was ardently longing for, and I dared to hope it would be mine, although I could see it only looming in the distance.

It happened that, on that day, M. D—— R—— had invited a large company to supper. I had, as a matter of course, to engross all conversation, and to give the fullest particulars of all that had taken place from the moment I received the order to place myself under arrest up to the time of my release from the 'bastarda'. M. Foscari was seated next to me, and the last part of my narrative was not, I suppose, particularly agreeable to him.

The account I gave of my adventures pleased everybody, and it was decided that the proveditore-generale must have the pleasure of hearing my tale from my own lips. I mentioned that hay was very plentiful in Casopo, and as that article was very scarce in Corfu, M. D—— R—— told me that I ought to seize the opportunity of making myself agreeable to the general by informing him of that circumstance without delay. I followed his advice the very next day, and was very well received, for his excellency immediately ordered a squad of men to go to the island and bring large quantities of hay to Corfu.

A few days later the Adjutant Minolto came to me in the coffee-house, and told me that the general wished to see me: this time I promptly obeyed his commands.

III

PROGRESS OF MY AMOUR—MY JOURNEY TO OTRANTO—I ENTER
THE SERVICE OF MADAME F.—A FORTUNATE EXCORIATION

The room I entered was full of people. His excellency, seeing me, smiled and drew upon me the attention of all his guests by saying aloud, "Here comes the young man who is a good judge of princes."

"My lord, I have become a judge of nobility by frequenting the society of men like you."

"The ladies are curious to know all you have done from the time of your escape from Corfu up to your return."

"Then you sentence me, monsignor, to make a public confession?"

"Exactly; but, as it is to be a confession, be careful not to omit the most insignificant circumstance, and suppose that I am not in the room."

"On the contrary, I wish to receive absolution only from your excellency. But my history will be a long one."

"If such is the case, your confessor gives you permission to be seated."

I gave all the particulars of my adventures, with the exception of my dalliance with the nymphs of the island.

"Your story is a very instructive one," observed the general.

"Yes, my lord, for the adventures shew that a young man is never so near his utter ruin than when, excited by some great passion, he finds himself able to minister to it, thanks to the gold in his purse."

I was preparing to take my leave, when the majordomo came to inform me that his excellency desired me to remain to supper. I had therefore the honour of a seat at his table, but not the pleasure of eating, for I was obliged to answer the questions addressed to me from all quarters, and I could not contrive to swallow a single mouthful. I was seated next to the Proto-Papa Bulgari, and I entreated his pardon for having ridiculed Deldimopulo's oracle. "It is nothing else but regular cheating," he said, "but it is very difficult to put a stop to it; it is an old custom."

A short time afterwards, Madame F—— whispered a few words to the general, who turned to me and said that he would be glad to hear me relate what had occurred to me in Constantinople with the wife of the Turk Yusuf, and at another friend's house, where I had seen bathing by moonlight. I was rather surprised at such an invitation, and told him that such frolics were not worth listening to, and the general not pressing me no more was said about it. But I was astonished at Madame F——'s indiscretion; she had no business to make my confidences public. I wanted her to be jealous of her own dignity, which I loved even more than her person.

Two or three days later, she said to me,

"Why did you refuse to tell your adventures in Constantinople before the general?"

"Because I do not wish everybody to know that you allow me to tell you such things. What I may dare, madam, to say to you when we are alone, I would certainly not say to you in public."

"And why not? It seems to me, on the contrary, that if you are silent in public out of respect for me, you ought to be all the more silent when we are alone."

"I wanted to amuse you, and have exposed myself to the danger of displeasing you, but I can assure you, madam, that I will not run such a risk again."

"I have no wish to pry into your intentions, but it strikes me that if your wish was to please me, you ought not to have run the risk of obtaining the opposite result. We take supper with the general this evening, and M. D—— R—— has been asked to bring you. I feel certain that the general will ask you again for your adventures in Constantinople, and this time you cannot refuse him."

M. D—— R—— came in and we went to the general's. I thought as we were driving along that, although Madame F—— seemed to have intended to humiliate me, I ought to accept it all as a favour of fortune, because, by compelling me to explain my refusal to the general; Madame F——had, at the same time, compelled me to a declaration of my feelings, which was not without importance.

The 'proveditore-generale' gave me a friendly welcome, and kindly handed me a letter which had come with the official dispatches from Constantinople. I bowed my thanks, and put the letter in my pocket: but he told me that he was himself a great lover of news, and that I could read my letter. I opened it; it was from Yusuf, who announced the death of Count de Bonneval. Hearing the name of the worthy Yusuf, the general asked me to tell him my adventure with his wife. I could not now refuse, and I began a story which amused and interested the general and his friends for an hour or so, but which was from beginning to end the work of my imagination.

Thus I continued to respect the privacy of Yusuf, to avoid implicating the good fame of Madame F——, and to shew myself in a light which was tolerably advantageous to me. My story, which was full of sentiment, did me a great deal of honour, and I felt very happy when I saw from the expression of Madame F——'s face that she was pleased with me, although somewhat surprised.

When we found ourselves again in her house she told me, in the presence of M. D—— R——, that the story I had related to the general was certainly very pretty, although purely imaginary, that she was not angry with me, because I had amused her, but that she could not help remarking my obstinacy in refusing compliance with her wishes. Then, turning to M. D—— R——, she said,

"M. Casanova pretends that if he had given an account of his meeting with Yusuf's wife without changing anything everybody would think that I allowed him to entertain me with indecent stories. I want you to give your opinion about it. Will you," she added, speaking to me, "be so good as to relate immediately the adventure in the same words which you have used when you told me of it?"

"Yes, madam, if you wish me to do so."

Stung to the quick by an indiscretion which, as I did not yet know women thoroughly, seemed to me without example, I cast all fears of displeasing to the winds, related the adventure with all the warmth of an impassioned poet, and without disguising or attenuating in the least the desires which the charms of the Greek beauty had inspired me with.

"Do you think," said M. D—— R—— to Madame F——, "that he ought to have related that adventure before all our friends as he has just related it to us?"

"If it be wrong for him to tell it in public, it is also wrong to tell it to me in private."

"You are the only judge of that: yes, if he has displeased you; no, if he has amused you. As for my own opinion, here it is: He has just now amused me very much, but he would have greatly displeased me if he had related the same adventure in public."

"Then," exclaimed Madame F——, "I must request you never to tell me in private anything that you cannot repeat in public."

"I promise, madam, to act always according to your wishes."

"It being understood," added M. D—— R——, smiling, "that madam reserves all rights of repealing that order whenever she may think fit."

I was vexed, but I contrived not to show it. A few minutes more, and we took leave of Madame F——.

I was beginning to understand that charming woman, and to dread the ordeal to which she would subject me. But love was stronger than fear, and, fortified with hope, I had the courage to endure the thorns, so as to gather the rose at the end of my sufferings. I was particularly pleased to find that M. D—— R—— was not jealous of me, even when she seemed to dare him to it. This was a point of the greatest importance.

A few days afterwards, as I was entertaining her on various subjects, she remarked how unfortunate it had been for me to enter the lazzaretto at Ancona without any money.

"In spite of my distress," I said, "I fell in love with a young and beautiful Greek slave, who very nearly contrived to make me break through all the sanitary laws."

"How so?"

"You are alone, madam, and I have not forgotten your orders."

"Is it a very improper story?"

"No: yet I would not relate it to you in public."

"Well," she said, laughing, "I repeal my order, as M. D—— R—— said I would. Tell me all about it."

I told my story, and, seeing that she was pensive, I exaggerated the misery I had felt at not being able to complete my conquest.

"What do you mean by your misery? I think that the poor girl was more to be pitied than you. You have never seen her since?"

"I beg your pardon, madam; I met her again, but I dare not tell you when or how."

"Now you must go on; it is all nonsense for you to stop. Tell me all; I expect you have been guilty of some black deed."

"Very far from it, madam, for it was a very sweet, although incomplete, enjoyment."

"Go on! But do not call things exactly by their names. It is not necessary to go into details."

Emboldened by the renewal of her order, I told her, without looking her in the face, of my meeting with the Greek slave in the presence of Bellino, and of the act which was cut short by the appearance of her master. When I had finished my story, Madame F—— remained silent, and I turned the conversation into a different channel, for though I felt myself on an excellent footing with her, I knew likewise that I had to proceed with great prudence. She was too young to have lowered herself before, and she would certainly look upon a connection with me as a lowering of her dignity.

Fortune which had always smiled upon me in the most hopeless cases, did not intend to ill-treat me on this occasion, and procured me, on that very same day, a favour of a very peculiar nature. My charming ladylove having pricked her finger rather severely, screamed loudly, and stretched her hand towards me, entreating me to suck the blood flowing from the wound. You may judge, dear reader, whether I was long in seizing that beautiful hand, and if you are, or if you have ever been in love, you will easily guess the manner in which I performed my delightful work. What is a kiss? Is it not an ardent desire to inhale a portion of the being we love? Was not the blood I was sucking from that charming wound a portion of the woman I worshipped? When I had completed my work, she thanked me affectionately, and told me to spit out the blood I had sucked.

"It is here," I said, placing my hand on my heart, "and God alone knows what happiness it has given me."

"You have drunk my blood with happiness! Are you then a cannibal?"

"I believe not, madam; but it would have been sacrilege in my eyes if I had suffered one single drop of your blood to be lost."

One evening, there was an unusually large attendance at M. D——R——'s assembly, and we were talking of the carnival which was near at hand. Everybody was regretting the lack of actors, and the impossibility of enjoying the pleasures of the theatre. I immediately offered to procure a good company at my expense, if the boxes were at once subscribed for, and the monopoly of the faro bank granted to me. No time was to be lost, for the carnival was approaching, and I had to go to Otranto to engage a troop. My proposal was accepted with great joy, and the proveditore-generale placed a felucca at my disposal. The boxes were all taken in three days, and a Jew took the pit, two nights a week excepted, which I reserved for my own profit.

The carnival being very long that year, I had every chance of success. It is said generally that the profession of theatrical manager is difficult, but, if that is the case, I have not found it so by experience, and am bound to affirm the contrary.

I left Corfu in the evening, and having a good breeze in my favour, I reached Otranto by day-break the following morning, without the oarsmen having had to row a stroke. The distance from Corfu to Otranto is only about fifteen leagues.

I had no idea of landing, owing to the quarantine which is always enforced for any ship or boat coming to Italy from the east. I only went to the parlour of the lazaretto, where, placed behind a grating, you can speak to any person who calls, and who must stand behind another grating placed opposite, at a distance of six feet.

As soon as I announced that I had come for the purpose of engaging a troupe of actors to perform in Corfu, the managers of the two companies then in Otranto came to the parlour to speak to me. I told them at once that I wished to see all the performers, one company at a time.

The two rival managers gave me then a very comic scene, each manager wanting the other to bring his troupe first. The harbour-master told me that the only way to settle the matter was to say myself which of the two companies I would see first: one was from Naples, the other from Sicily. Not knowing either I gave the preference to the first. Don Fastidio, the manager, was very vexed, while Battipaglia, the director of the second, was delighted because he hoped that, after seeing the Neapolitan troupe, I would engage his own.

An hour afterwards, Fastidio returned with all his performers, and my surprise may be imagined when amongst them I recognized Petronio and his sister Marina, who, the moment she saw me, screamed for joy, jumped over the grating, and threw herself in my arms. A terrible hubbub followed, and high words passed between Fastidio and the harbour-master. Marina being in the service of Fastidio, the captain compelled him to confine her to the lazaretto, where she would have to perform quarantine at his expense. The poor girl cried bitterly, but I could not remedy her imprudence.

I put a stop to the quarrel by telling Fastidio to shew me all his people, one after the other. Petronio belonged to his company, and performed the lovers. He told me that he had a letter for me from Therese. I was also glad to see a Venetian of my acquaintance who played the pantaloon in the pantomime, three tolerably pretty actresses, a pulcinella, and a scaramouch. Altogether, the troupe was a decent one.

I told Fastidio to name the lowest salary he wanted for all his company, assuring him that I would give the preference to his rival, if he should ask me too much.

"Sir," he answered, "we are twenty, and shall require six rooms with ten beds, one sitting-room for all of us, and thirty Neapolitan ducats a day, all travelling expenses paid. Here is my stock of plays, and we will perform those that you may choose."

Thinking of poor Marina who would have to remain in the lazaretto before she could reappear on the stage at Otranto, I told Fastidio to get the contract ready, as I wanted to go away immediately.

I had scarcely pronounced these words than war broke out again between the manager-elect and his unfortunate competitor. Battipaglia, in his rage, called Marina a harlot, and said that she had arranged beforehand with Fastidio to violate the rules of the lazaretto in order to compel me to choose their troupe. Petronio, taking his sister's part, joined Fastidio, and the unlucky Battipaglia was dragged outside and treated to a generous dose of blows and fisticuffs, which was not exactly the thing to console him for a lost engagement.

Soon afterwards, Petronio brought me Therese's letter. She was ruining the duke, getting rich accordingly, and waiting for me in Naples.

Everything being ready towards evening, I left Otranto with twenty actors, and six large trunks containing their complete wardrobes. A light breeze which was blowing from the south might have carried us to Corfu in ten hours, but when we had sailed about one hour my cayabouchiri informed me that he could see by the moonlight a ship which might prove to be a corsair, and get hold of us. I was unwilling to risk anything, so I ordered them to lower the sails and return to Otranto. At day-break we sailed again with a good westerly wind, which would also have taken us to Corfu; but after we had gone two or three hours, the captain pointed out to me a brigantine, evidently a pirate, for she was shaping her course so as to get to windward of us. I told him to change the course, and to go by starboard, to see if the brigantine would follow us, but she immediately imitated our manoeuvre. I could not go back to Otranto, and I had no wish to go to Africa, so I ordered the men to shape our course, so as to land on the coast of Calabria, by hard rowing and at the nearest point. The sailors, who were frightened to death, communicated their fears to my comedians, and soon I heard nothing but weeping and sobbing. Every one of them was calling earnestly upon some saint, but not one single prayer to God did I hear. The bewailings of scaramouch, the dull and spiritless despair of Fastidio, offered a picture which would have made me laugh heartily if the danger had been imaginary and not real. Marina alone was cheerful and happy, because she did not realize the danger we were running, and she laughed at the terror of the crew and of her companions.

A strong breeze sprang up towards evening, so I ordered them to clap on all sail and scud before the wind, even if it should get stronger.

In order to escape the pirate, I had made up my mind to cross the gulf. We took the wind through the night, and in the morning we were eighty miles from Corfu, which I determined to reach by rowing. We were in the middle of the gulf, and the sailors were worn out with fatigue, but I had no longer any fear. A gale began to blow from the north, and in less than an hour it was blowing so hard that we were compelled to sail close to the wind in a fearful manner. The felucca looked every moment as if it must capsize. Every one looked terrified but kept complete silence, for I had enjoined it on penalty of death. In spite of our dangerous position, I could not help laughing when I heard the sobs of the cowardly scaramouch. The helmsman was a man of great nerve, and the gale being steady I felt we would reach Corfu without mishap. At day-break we sighted the town, and at nine in the morning we landed at Mandrachia. Everybody was surprised to see us arrive that way.

As soon as my company was landed, the young officers naturally came to inspect the actresses, but they did not find them very desirable, with the exception of Marina, who received uncomplainingly the news that I could not renew my acquaintance with her. I felt certain that she would not lack admirers. But my actresses, who had appeared ugly at the landing, produced a very different effect on the stage, and particularly the pantaloon's wife. M. Duodo, commander of a man-of-war, called upon her, and, finding master pantaloon intolerant on the subject of his better-half, gave him a few blows with his cane. Fastidio informed me the next day that the pantaloon and his wife refused to perform any more, but I made them alter their mind by giving them a benefit night.

The pantaloon's wife was much applauded, but she felt insulted because, in the midst of the applause, the pit called out, "Bravo, Duodo!" She presented herself to the general in his own box, in which I was generally, and complained of the manner in which she was treated. The general promised her, in my name, another benefit night for the close of the carnival, and I was of course compelled to ratify his promise. The fact is, that, to satisfy the greedy actors, I abandoned to my comedians, one by one, the seventeen nights I had reserved for myself. The benefit I gave to Marina was at the special request of Madame F——, who had taken her into great favour since she had had the honour of breakfasting alone with M. D—— R—— in a villa outside of the city.

My generosity cost me four hundred sequins, but the faro bank brought me a thousand and more, although I never held the cards, my management of the theatre taking up all my time. My manner with the actresses gained me great kindness; it was clearly seen that I carried on no intrigue with any of them, although I had every facility for doing so. Madame F—— complimented me, saying that she had not entertained such a good opinion of my discretion. I was too busy through the carnival to think of love, even of the passion which filled my heart. It was only at the beginning of Lent, and after the departure of the comedians, that I could give rein to my feelings.

One morning Madame F—— sent, a messenger who, summoned me to her presence. It was eleven o'clock; I immediately went to her, and enquired what I could do for her service.

"I wanted to see you," she said, "to return the two hundred sequins which you lent me so nobly. Here they are; be good enough to give me back my note of hand."

"Your note of hand, madam, is no longer in my possession. I have deposited it in a sealed envelope with the notary who, according to this receipt of his, can return it only to you."

"Why did you not keep it yourself?"

"Because I was afraid of losing it, or of having it stolen. And in the event of my death I did not want such a document to fall into any other hands but yours."

"A great proof of your extreme delicacy, certainly, but I think you ought to have reserved the right of taking it out of the notary's custody yourself."

"I did not forsee the possibility of calling for it myself."

"Yet it was a very likely thing. Then I can send word to the notary to transmit it to me?"

"Certainly, madam; you alone can claim it."

She sent to the notary, who brought the himself.

She tore the envelope open, and found only a piece of paper besmeared with ink, quite illegible, except her own name, which had not been touched.

"You have acted," she said, "most nobly; but you must agree with me that I cannot be certain that this piece of paper is really my note of hand, although I see my name on it."

"True, madam; and if you are not certain of it, I confess myself in the wrong."

"I must be certain of it, and I am so; but you must grant that I could not swear to it."

"Granted, madam."

During the following days it struck me that her manner towards me was singularly altered. She never received me in her dishabille, and I had to wait with great patience until her maid had entirely dressed her before being admitted into her presence.

If I related any story, any adventure, she pretended not to understand, and affected not to see the point of an anecdote or a jest; very often she would purposely not look at me, and then I was sure to relate badly. If M. D—— R—— laughed at something I had just said, she would ask what he was laughing for, and when he had told her, she would say it was insipid or dull. If one of her bracelets became unfastened, I offered to fasten it again, but either she would not give me so much trouble, or I did not understand the fastening, and the maid was called to do it. I could not help shewing my vexation, but she did not seem to take the slightest notice of it. If M. D—— R—— excited me to say something amusing or witty, and I did not speak immediately, she would say that my budget was empty, laughing, and adding that the wit of poor M. Casanova was worn out. Full of rage, I would plead guilty by my silence to her taunting accusation, but I was thoroughly miserable, for I did not see any cause for that extraordinary change in her feelings, being conscious that I had not given her any motive for it. I wanted to shew her openly my indifference and contempt, but whenever an opportunity offered, my courage would forsake me, and I would let it escape.

One evening M. D—— R—— asking me whether I had often been in love, I answered,

"Three times, my lord."

"And always happily, of course."

"Always unhappily. The first time, perhaps, because, being an ecclesiastic, I durst not speak openly of my love. The second, because a cruel, unexpected event compelled me to leave the woman I loved at the very moment in which my happiness would have been complete. The third time, because the feeling of pity, with which I inspired the beloved object, induced her to cure me of my passion, instead of crowning my felicity."

"But what specific remedies did she use to effect your cure?"

"She has ceased to be kind."

"I understand she has treated you cruelly, and you call that pity, do you? You are mistaken."

"Certainly," said Madame F——, "a woman may pity the man she loves, but she would not think of ill-treating him to cure him of his passion. That woman has never felt any love for you."

"I cannot, I will not believe it, madam."

"But are you cured?"

"Oh! thoroughly; for when I happen to think of her, I feel nothing but indifference and coldness. But my recovery was long."

"Your convalescence lasted, I suppose, until you fell in love with another."

"With another, madam? I thought I had just told you that the third time I loved was the last."

A few days after that conversation, M. D—— R—— told me that Madame F—— was not well, that he could not keep her company, and that I ought to go to her, as he was sure she would be glad to see me. I obeyed, and told Madame F—— what M. D—— R—— had said. She was lying on a sofa. Without looking at me, she told me she was feverish, and would not ask me to remain with her, because I would feel weary.

"I could not experience any weariness in your society, madam; at all events, I can leave you only by your express command, and, in that case, I must spend the next four hours in your ante-room, for M. D—— R—— has told me to wait for him here."

"If so, you may take a seat."

Her cold and distant manner repelled me, but I loved her, and I had never seen her so beautiful, a slight fever animating her complexion which was then truly dazzling in its beauty. I kept where I was, dumb and as motionless as a statue, for a quarter of an hour. Then she rang for her maid, and asked me to leave her alone for a moment. I was called back soon after, and she said to me,

"What has become of your cheerfulness?"

"If it has disappeared, madam, it can only be by your will. Call it back, and you will see it return in full force."

"What must I do to obtain that result?"

"Only be towards me as you were when I returned from Casopo. I have been disagreeable to you for the last four months, and as I do not know why, I feel deeply grieved."

"I am always the same: in what do you find me changed?"

"Good heavens! In everything, except in beauty. But I have taken my decision."

"And what is it?"

"To suffer in silence, without allowing any circumstance to alter the feelings with which you have inspired me; to wish ardently to convince you of my perfect obedience to your commands; to be ever ready to give you fresh proofs of my devotion."

"I thank you, but I cannot imagine what you can have to suffer in silence on my account. I take an interest in you, and I always listen with pleasure to your adventures. As a proof of it, I am extremely curious to hear the history of your three loves."

I invented on the spot three purely imaginary stories, making a great display of tender sentiments and of ardent love, but without alluding to amorous enjoyment, particularly when she seemed to expect me to do so. Sometimes delicacy, sometimes respect or duty, interfered to prevent the crowning pleasure, and I took care to observe, at such moments of disappointment, that a true lover does not require that all important item to feel perfectly happy. I could easily see that her imagination was travelling farther than my narrative, and that my reserve was agreeable to her. I believed I knew her nature well enough to be certain that I was taking the best road to induce her to follow me where I wished to lead her. She expressed a sentiment which moved me deeply, but I was careful not to shew it. We were talking of my third love, of the woman who, out of pity, had undertaken to cure me, and she remarked,

"If she truly loved you, she may have wished not to cure you, but to cure herself."

On the day following this partial reconciliation, M. F——, her husband, begged my commanding officer, D—— R——, to let me go with him to Butintro for an excursion of three days, his own adjutant being seriously ill.

Butintro is seven miles from Corfu, almost opposite to that city; it is the nearest point to the island from the mainland. It is not a fortress, but only a small village of Epirus, or Albania, as it is now called, and belonging to the Venetians. Acting on the political axiom that "neglected right is lost right," the Republic sends every year four galleys to Butintro with a gang of galley slaves to fell trees, cut them, and load them on the galleys, while the military keep a sharp look-out to prevent them from escaping to Turkey and becoming Mussulmans. One of the four galleys was commanded by M. F—— who, wanting an adjutant for the occasion, chose me.

I went with him, and on the fourth day we came back to Corfu with a large provision of wood. I found M. D—— R—— alone on the terrace of his palace. It was Good Friday. He seemed thoughtful, and, after a silence of a few minutes, he spoke the following words, which I can never forget:

"M. F——, whose adjutant died yesterday, has just been entreating me to give you to him until he can find another officer. I have told him that I had no right to dispose of your person, and that he, ought to apply to you, assuring him that, if you asked me leave to go with him, I would not raise any objection, although I require two adjutants. Has he not mentioned the matter to you?"

"No, monsignor, he has only tendered me his thanks for having accompanied him to Butintro, nothing else."

"He is sure to speak to you about it. What do you intend to say?"

"Simply that I will never leave the service of your excellency without your express command to do so."

"I never will give you such an order."

As M. D—— R—— was saying the last word, M. and Madame F—— came in. Knowing that the conversation would most likely turn upon the subject which had just been broached, I hurried out of the room. In less than a quarter of an hour I was sent for, and M. F—— said to me, confidentially,

"Well, M. Casanova, would you not be willing to live with me as my adjutant?"

"Does his excellency dismiss me from his service?"

"Not at all," observed M. D—— R——, "but I leave you the choice."

"My lord, I could not be guilty of ingratitude."

And I remained there standing, uneasy, keeping my eyes on the ground, not even striving to conceal my mortification, which was, after all, very natural in such a position. I dreaded looking at Madame F——, for I knew that she could easily guess all my feelings. An instant after, her foolish husband coldly remarked that I should certainly have a more fatiguing service with him than with M. D—— R——, and that, of course, it was more honourable to serve the general governor of the galeazze than a simple sopra-committo. I was on the point of answering, when Madame F—— said, in a graceful and easy manner, "M. Casanova is right," and she changed the subject. I left the room, revolving in my mind all that had just taken place.

My conclusion was that M. F—— had asked M. D—— R—— to let me go with him at the suggestion of his wife, or, at least with her consent, and it was highly flattering to my love and to my vanity. But

I was bound in honour not to accept the post, unless I had a perfect assurance that it would not be disagreeable to my present patron. "I will accept," I said to myself, "if M. D—— R—— tells me positively that I shall please him by doing so. It is for M. F to make him say it."

On the same night I had the honour of offering my arm to Madame F—— during the procession which takes place in commemoration of the death of our Lord and Saviour, which was then attended on foot by all the nobility. I expected she would mention the matter, but she did not. My love was in despair, and through the night I could not close my eyes. I feared she had been offended by my refusal, and was overwhelmed with grief. I passed the whole of the next day without breaking my fast, and did not utter a single word during the evening reception. I felt very unwell, and I had an attack of fever which kept me in bed on Easter Sunday. I was very weak on the Monday, and intended to remain in my room, when a messenger from Madame F—— came to inform me that she wished to see me. I told the messenger not to say that he had found me in bed, and dressing myself rapidly I hurried to her house. I entered her room, pale, looking very ill: yet she did not enquire after my health, and kept silent a minute or two, as if she had been trying to recollect what she had to say to me.

"Ah! yes, you are aware that our adjutant is dead, and that we want to replace him. My husband, who has a great esteem for you, and feels that M. D—— R—— leaves you perfectly free to make your choice, has taken the singular fancy that you will come, if I ask you myself to do us that pleasure. Is he mistaken? If you would come to us, you would have that room."

She was pointing to a room adjoining the chamber in which she slept, and so situated that, to see her in every part of her room, I should not even require to place myself at the window.

"M. D—— R——," she continued, "will not love you less, and as he will see you here every day, he will not be likely to forget his interest in your welfare. Now, tell me, will you come or not?"

"I wish I could, madam, but indeed I cannot."

"You cannot? That is singular. Take a seat, and tell me what there is to prevent you, when, in accepting my offer, you are sure to please M. D—— R—— as well as us."

"If I were certain of it, I would accept immediately; but all I have heard from his lips was that he left me free to make a choice."

"Then you are afraid to grieve him, if you come to us?"

"It might be, and for nothing on earth. . ."

"I am certain of the contrary."

"Will you be so good as to obtain that he says so to me himself?"

"And then you will come?"

"Oh, madam! that very minute!"

But the warmth of my exclamation might mean a great deal, and I turned my head round so as not to embarrass her. She asked me to give her her mantle to go to church, and we went out. As we were going down the stairs, she placed her ungloved hand upon mine. It was the first time that she had granted me such a favour, and it seemed to me a good omen. She took off her hand, asking me whether I was feverish. "Your hand," she said, "is burning."

When we left the church, M. D—— R——'s carriage happened to pass, and I assisted her to get in, and as soon as she had gone, hurried to my room in order to breathe freely and to enjoy all the felicity which filled my soul; for I no longer doubted her love for me, and I knew that, in this case, M. D—— R—— was not likely to refuse her anything.

What is love? I have read plenty of ancient verbiage on that subject, I have read likewise most of what has been said by modern writers, but neither all that has been said, nor what I have thought about it, when I was young and now that I am no longer so, nothing, in fact, can make me agree that love is a trifling vanity. It is a sort of madness, I grant that, but a madness over which philosophy is entirely powerless; it is a disease to which man is exposed at all times, no matter at what age, and which cannot be cured, if he is attacked by it in his old age. Love being sentiment which cannot be explained! God of all nature!—bitter and sweet feeling! Love!—charming monster which cannot be fathomed! God who, in the midst of all the thorns with which thou plaguest us, strewest so many roses on our path that, without thee, existence and death would be united and blended together!

Two days afterwards, M. D—— R——, told me to go and take orders from M. F—— on board his galley, which was ready for a five or six days' voyage. I quickly packed a few things, and called for my new patron who received me with great joy. We took our departure without seeing madam, who was not yet visible. We returned on the sixth day, and I went to establish myself in my new home, for, as I was preparing to go to M. D—— R——, to take his orders, after our landing, he came himself, and after asking M. F—— and me whether we were pleased with each other, he said to me,

"Casanova, as you suit each other so well, you may be certain that you will greatly please me by remaining in the service of M. F."

I obeyed respectfully, and in less than one hour I had taken possession of my new quarters. Madame F—— told me how delighted she was to see that great affair ended according to her wishes, and I answered with a deep reverence.

I found myself like the salamander, in the very heart of the fire for which I had been longing so ardently.

Almost constantly in the presence of Madame F——, dining often alone with her, accompanying her in her walks, even when M. D—— R——was not with us, seeing her from my room, or conversing with her in her chamber, always reserved and attentive without pretension, the first night passed by without any change being brought about by that constant intercourse. Yet I was full of hope, and to keep up my courage I imagined that love was not yet powerful enough to conquer her pride. I expected everything from some lucky chance, which I promised myself to improve as soon as it should present itself, for I was persuaded that a lover is lost if he does not catch fortune by the forelock.

But there was one circumstance which annoyed me. In public, she seized every opportunity of treating me with distinction, while, when we were alone, it was exactly the reverse. In the eyes of the world I had all the appearance of a happy lover, but I would rather have had less of the appearance of happiness and more of the reality. My love for her was disinterested; vanity had no share in my feelings.

One day, being alone with me, she said,

"You have enemies, but I silenced them last night."

"They are envious, madam, and they would pity me if they could read the secret pages of my heart. You could easily deliver me from those enemies."

"How can you be an object of pity for them, and how could I deliver you from them?"

"They believe me happy, and I am miserable; you would deliver me from them by ill-treating me in their presence."

"Then you would feel my bad treatment less than the envy of the wicked?"

"Yes, madam, provided your bad treatment in public were compensated by your kindness when we are alone, for there is no vanity in the happiness I feel in belonging to you. Let others pity me, I will be happy on condition that others are mistaken."

"That's a part that I can never play."

I would often be indiscreet enough to remain behind the curtain of the window in my room, looking at her when she thought herself perfectly certain that nobody saw her; but the liberty I was thus guilty of never proved of great advantage to me. Whether it was because she doubted my discretion or from habitual reserve, she was so particular that, even when I saw her in bed, my longing eyes never could obtain a sight of anything but her head.

One day, being present in her room while her maid was cutting off the points of her long and beautiful hair, I amused myself in picking up all those pretty bits, and put them all, one after the other, on her toilettable, with the exception of one small lock which I slipped into my pocket, thinking that she had not taken any notice of my keeping it; but the moment we were alone she told me quietly, but rather too seriously, to take out of my pocket the hair I had picked up from the floor. Thinking she was going too far, and such rigour appearing to me as cruel as it was unjust and absurd, I obeyed, but threw the hair on the toilet-table with an air of supreme contempt.

"Sir, you forget yourself."

"No, madam, I do not, for you might have feigned not to have observed such an innocent theft."

"Feigning is tiresome."

"Was such petty larceny a very great crime?"

"No crime, but it was an indication of feelings which you have no right to entertain for me."

"Feelings which you are at liberty not to return, madam, but which hatred or pride can alone forbid my heart to experience. If you had a heart you would not be the victim of either of those two fearful passions, but you have only head, and it must be a very wicked head, judging by the care it takes to heap humiliation upon me. You have surprised my secret, madam, you may use it as you think proper, but in the meantime I have learned to know you thoroughly. That knowledge will prove more useful than your discovery, for perhaps it will help me to become wiser."

After this violent tirade I left her, and as she did not call me back retired to my room. In the hope that sleep would bring calm, I undressed and went to bed. In such moments a lover hates the object of his love, and his heart distils only contempt and hatred. I could not go to sleep, and when I was sent for at supper-time I answered that I was ill. The night passed off without my eyes being visited by sleep, and feeling weak and low I thought I would wait to see what ailed me, and refused to have my dinner, sending word that I was still very unwell. Towards evening I felt my heart leap for joy when I heard my beautiful lady-love enter my room. Anxiety, want of food and sleep, gave me truly the appearance of being ill, and I was delighted that it should be so. I sent her away very soon, by telling her with perfect indifference that it was nothing but a bad headache, to which I was subject, and that repose and diet would effect a speedy cure.

But at eleven o'clock she came back with her friend, M. D—— R——, and coming to my bed she said, affectionately,

"What ails you, my poor Casanova?"

"A very bad headache, madam, which will be cured to-morrow."

"Why should you wait until to-morrow? You must get better at once. I have ordered a basin of broth and two new-laid eggs for you."

"Nothing, madam; complete abstinence can alone cure me."

"He is right," said M. D—— R——, "I know those attacks."

I shook my head slightly. M. D—— R—— having just then turned round to examine an engraving, she took my hand, saying that she would like me to drink some broth, and I felt that she was giving me a small parcel. She went to look at the engraving with M. D—— R——.

I opened the parcel, but feeling that it contained hair, I hurriedly concealed it under the bed-clothes: at the same moment the blood rushed to my head with such violence that it actually frightened me. I begged for some water, she came to me, with M. D—— R——, and then were both frightened to see me so red, when they had seen me pale and weak only one minute before.

Madame F—— gave me a glass of water in which she put some Eau des carmes which instantly acted as a violent emetic. Two or three minutes after I felt better, and asked for something to eat. Madame F—— smiled. The servant came in with the broth and the eggs, and while I was eating I told the history of Pandolfin. M. D—— R—— thought it was all a miracle, and I could read, on the countenance of the charming woman, love, affection, and repentance. If M. D—— R—— had not been present, it would have been the moment of my happiness, but I felt certain that I should not have long to wait. M. D—— R—— told Madame F—— that, if he had not seen me so sick, he would have believed my illness to be all sham, for he did not think it possible for anyone to rally so rapidly.

"It is all owing to my Eau des carmes," said Madame F——, looking at me, "and I will leave you my bottle."

"No, madam, be kind enough to take it with you, for the water would have no virtue without your presence."

"I am sure of that," said M. D—— R——, "so I will leave you here with your patient."

"No, no, he must go to sleep now."

I slept all night, but in my happy dreams I was with her, and the reality itself would hardly have procured me greater enjoyment than I had during my happy slumbers. I saw I had taken a very long stride forward, for twenty-four hours of abstinence gave me the right to speak to her openly of my love, and the gift of her hair was an irrefutable confession of her own feelings.

On the following day, after presenting myself before M. F——, I went to have a little chat with the maid, to wait until her mistress was visible, which was not long, and I had the pleasure of hearing her laugh when the maid told her I was there. As soon as I went in, without giving me time to say a single word, she told me how delighted she was to see me looking so well, and advised me to call upon M. D——R——.

It is not only in the eyes of a lover, but also in those of every man of taste, that a woman is a thousand times more lovely at the moment she comes out of the arms of Morpheus than when she has completed her toilet. Around Madame F—— more brilliant beams were blazing than around the sun when he leaves the embrace of Aurora. Yet the most beautiful woman thinks as much of her toilet as the one who cannot do without it—very likely because more human creatures possess the more they want.

In the order given to me by Madame F—— to call on M. D—— R——, I saw another reason to be certain of approaching happiness, for I thought that, by dismissing me so quickly, she had only tried to postpone the consummation which I might have pressed upon her, and which she could not have refused.

Rich in the possession of her hair, I held a consultation with my love to decide what I ought to do with it, for Madame F——, very likely in her wish to atone for the miserly sentiment which had refused me a small bit, had given me a splendid lock, full a yard and a half long. Having thought it over, I called upon a Jewish confectioner whose daughter was a skilful embroiderer, and I made her embroider before me, on a bracelet of green satin, the four initial letters of our names, and make a very thin chain with the remainder. I had a piece of black ribbon added to one end of the chain, in the shape of a sliding noose, with which I could easily strangle myself if ever love should reduce me to despair, and I passed it round my neck. As I did not want to lose even the smallest particle of so precious a treasure, I cut with a pair of scissors all the small bits which were left, and devoutly gathered them together. Then I reduced them into a fine powder, and ordered the Jewish confectioner to mix the powder in my presence with a paste made of amber, sugar, vanilla, angelica, alkermes and storax, and I waited until the comfits prepared with that mixture were ready. I had some more made with the same composition, but without any hair; I put the first in a beautiful sweetmeat box of fine crystal, and the second in a tortoise-shell box.

From the day when, by giving me her hair, Madame F—— had betrayed the secret feelings of her heart, I no longer lost my time in relating stories or adventures; I only spoke to her of my cove, of my ardent desires; I told her that she must either banish me from her presence, or crown my happiness, but the cruel, charming woman would not accept that alternative. She answered that happiness could not be obtained by offending every moral law, and by swerving from our duties. If I threw myself at her feet to obtain by anticipation her forgiveness for the loving violence I intended to use against her, she would repulse me more powerfully than if she had had the strength of a female Hercules, for she would say, in a voice full of sweetness and affection,

"My friend, I do not entreat you to respect my weakness, but be generous enough to spare me for the sake of all the love I feel for you."

"What! you love me, and you refuse to make me happy! It is impossible! it is unnatural. You compel me to believe that you do not love me. Only allow me to press my lips one moment upon your lips, and I ask no more."

"No, dearest, no; it would only excite the ardour of your desires, shake my resolution, and we should then find ourselves more miserable than we are now."

Thus did she every day plunge me in despair, and yet she complained that my wit was no longer brilliant in society, that I had lost that elasticity of spirits which had pleased her so much after my arrival from Constantinople. M. D——R——, who often jestingly waged war against me, used to say that I was getting thinner and thinner every day. Madame F—— told me one day that my sickly looks were very disagreeable to her, because wicked tongues would not fail to say that she treated me with cruelty. Strange, almost unnatural thought! On it I composed an idyll which I cannot read, even now, without feeling tears in my eyes.

"What!" I answered, "you acknowledge your cruelty towards me? You are afraid of the world guessing all your heartless rigour, and yet you continue to enjoy it! You condemn me unmercifully to the torments of Tantalus! You would be delighted to see me gay, cheerful, happy, even at the expense of a judgment by which the world would find you guilty of a supposed but false kindness towards me, and yet you refuse me even the slightest favours!"

"I do not mind people believing anything, provided it is not true."

"What a contrast! Would it be possible for me not to love you, for you to feel nothing for me? Such contradictions strike me as unnatural. But you are growing thinner yourself, and I am dying. It must be so; we shall both die before long, you of consumption, I of exhausting decline; for I am now reduced to enjoying your shadow during the day, during the night, always, everywhere, except when I am in your presence."

At that passionate declaration, delivered with all the ardour of an excited lover, she was surprised, deeply moved, and I thought that the happy hour had struck. I folded her in my arms, and was already tasting the first fruits of enjoyment. . . The sentinel knocked twice! . . . Oh! fatal mischance! I recovered my composure and stood in front of her. . . M. D—— R—— made his appearance, and this time he found me in so cheerful a mood that he remained with us until one o'clock in the morning.

My comfits were beginning to be the talk of our society. M. D—— R——, Madame F——, and I were the only ones who had a box full of them. I was stingy with them, and no one durst beg any from me, because I had said that they were very expensive, and that in all Corfu there was no confectioner who could make or physician who could analyse them. I never gave one out of my crystal box, and Madame F. remarked it. I certainly did not believe them to be amorous philtre, and I was very far from supposing that the addition of the hair made them taste more delicious; but a superstition, the offspring of my love, caused me to cherish them, and it made me happy to think that a small portion of the woman I worshipped was thus becoming a part of my being.

Influenced perhaps by some secret sympathy, Madame F. was exceedingly fond of the comfits. She asserted before all her friends that they were the universal panacea, and knowing herself perfect mistress of the inventor, she did not enquire after the secret of the composition. But having observed that I gave away only the comfits which I kept in my tortoise-shell box, and that I never eat any but those from the crystal box, she one day asked me what reason I had for that. Without taking time to think, I told her that in those I kept for myself there was a certain ingredient which made the partaker love her.

"I do not believe it," she answered; "but are they different from those I eat myself?"

"They are exactly the same, with the exception of the ingredient I have just mentioned, which has been put only in mine."

"Tell me what the ingredient is."

"It is a secret which I cannot reveal to you."

"Then I will never eat any of your comfits."

Saying which, she rose, emptied her box, and filled it again with chocolate drops; and for the next few days she was angry with me, and avoided my company. I felt grieved, I became low-spirited, but I could not make up my mind to tell her that I was eating her hair!

She enquired why I looked so sad.

"Because you refuse to take my comfits."

"You are master of your secret, and I am mistress of my diet."

"That is my reward for having taken you into my confidence."

And I opened my box, emptied its contents in my hand, and swallowed the whole of them, saying, "Two more doses like this, and I shall die mad with love for you. Then you will be revenged for my reserve. Farewell, madam."

She called me back, made me take a seat near her, and told me not to commit follies which would make her unhappy; that I knew how much she loved me, and that it was not owing to the effect of any drug. "To prove to you," she added, "that you do not require anything of the sort to be loved, here is a token of my affection." And she offered me her lovely lips, and upon them mine remained pressed until I was compelled to draw a breath. I threw myself at her feet, with tears of love and gratitude blinding my eyes, and told her that I would confess my crime, if she would promise to forgive me.

"Your crime! You frighten me. Yes, I forgive you, but speak quickly, and tell me all."

"Yes, everything. My comfits contain your hair reduced to a powder. Here on my arm, see this bracelet on which our names are written with your hair, and round my neck this chain of the same material, which will help me to destroy my own life when your love fails me. Such is my crime, but I would not have been guilty of it, if I had not loved you."

She smiled, and, bidding me rise from my kneeling position, she told me that I was indeed the most criminal of men, and she wiped away my tears, assuring me that I should never have any reason to strangle myself with the chain.

After that conversation, in which I had enjoyed the sweet nectar of my divinity's first kiss, I had the courage to behave in a very different manner. She could see the ardour which consumed me; perhaps the same fire burned in her veins, but I abstained from any attack.

"What gives you," she said one day, "the strength to control yourself?"

"After the kiss which you granted to me of your own accord, I felt that I ought not to wish any favour unless your heart gave it as freely. You cannot imagine the happiness that kiss has given me."

"I not imagine it, you ungrateful man! Which of us has given that happiness?"

"Neither you nor I, angel of my soul! That kiss so tender, so sweet, was the child of love!"

"Yes, dearest, of love, the treasures of which are inexhaustible."

The words were scarcely spoken, when our lips were engaged in happy concert. She held me so tight against her bosom that I could not use my hands to secure other pleasures, but I felt myself perfectly happy. After that delightful skirmish, I asked her whether we were never to go any further.

"Never, dearest friend, never. Love is a child which must be amused with trifles; too substantial food would kill it."

"I know love better than you; it requires that substantial food, and unless it can obtain it, love dies of exhaustion. Do not refuse me the consolation of hope."

"Hope as much as you please, if it makes you happy."

"What should I do, if I had no hope? I hope, because I know you have a heart."

"Ah! yes. Do you recollect the day, when, in your anger, you told me that I had only a head, but no heart, thinking you were insulting me grossly!"

"Oh! yes, I recollect it."

"How heartily I laughed, when I had time to think! Yes, dearest, I have a heart, or I should not feel as happy as I feel now. Let us keep our happiness, and be satisfied with it, as it is, without wishing for anything more."

Obedient to her wishes, but every day more deeply enamoured, I was in hope that nature at last would prove stronger than prejudice, and would cause a fortunate crisis. But, besides nature, fortune was my friend, and I owed my happiness to an accident.

Madame F. was walking one day in the garden, leaning on M. D——R——'s arm, and was caught by a large rose-bush, and the prickly thorns left a deep cut on her leg. M. D—— R—— bandaged the wound with his handkerchief, so as to stop the blood which was flowing abundantly, and she had to be carried home in a palanquin.

In Corfu, wounds on the legs are dangerous when they are not well attended to, and very often the wounded are compelled to leave the city to be cured.

Madame F—— was confined to her bed, and my lucky position in the house condemned me to remain constantly at her orders. I saw her every minute; but, during the first three days, visitors succeeded each other without intermission, and I never was alone with her. In the evening, after everybody had gone, and her husband had retired to his own apartment, M. D—— R—— remained another hour, and for the sake of propriety I had to take my leave at the same time that he did. I had much more liberty before the accident, and I told her so half seriously, half jestingly. The next day, to make up for my disappointment, she contrived a moment of happiness for me.

An elderly surgeon came every morning to dress her wound, during which operation her maid only was present, but I used to go, in my morning dishabille, to the girl's room, and to wait there, so as to be the first to hear how my dear one was.

That morning, the girl came to tell me to go in as the surgeon was dressing the wound.

"See, whether my leg is less inflamed."

"To give an opinion, madam, I ought to have seen it yesterday."

"True. I feel great pain, and I am afraid of erysipelas."

"Do not be afraid, madam," said the surgeon, "keep your bed, and I answer for your complete recovery."

The surgeon being busy preparing a poultice at the other end of the room, and the maid out, I enquired whether she felt any hardness in the calf of the leg, and whether the inflammation went up the limb; and naturally, my eyes and my hands kept pace with my questions. . . I saw no inflammation, I felt no hardness, but. . . and the lovely patient hurriedly let the curtain fall, smiling, and allowing me to take a sweet kiss, the perfume of which I had not enjoyed for many days. It was a sweet moment; a delicious ecstacy. From her mouth my lips descended to her wound, and satisfied in that moment that my kisses were the best of medicines, I would have kept my lips there, if the noise made by the maid coming back had not compelled me to give up my delightful occupation.

When we were left alone, burning with intense desires, I entreated her to grant happiness at least to my eyes.

"I feel humiliated," I said to her, "by the thought that the felicity I have just enjoyed was only a theft."

"But supposing you were mistaken?"

The next day I was again present at the dressing of the wound, and as soon as the surgeon had left, she asked me to arrange her pillows, which I did at once. As if to make that pleasant office easier, she raised the bedclothes to support herself, and she thus gave me a sight of beauties which intoxicated my eyes, and I protracted the easy operation without her complaining of my being too slow.

When I had done I was in a fearful state, and I threw myself in an arm-chair opposite her bed, half dead, in a sort of trance. I was looking at that lovely being who, almost artless, was continually granting me greater and still greater favours, and yet never allowed me to reach the goal for which I was so ardently longing.

"What are you thinking of?" she said.

"Of the supreme felicity I have just been enjoying."

"You are a cruel man."

"No, I am not cruel, for, if you love me, you must not blush for your indulgence. You must know, too, that, loving you passionately, I must not suppose that it is to be a surprise that I am indebted for my happiness in the enjoyment of the most ravishing sights, for if I owed it only to mere chance I should be compelled to believe that any other man in my position might have had the same happiness, and such an idea would be misery to me. Let me be indebted to you for having proved to me this morning how much enjoyment I can derive from one of my senses. Can you be angry with my eyes?"

"Yes."

"They belong to you; tear them out."

The next day, the moment the doctor had gone, she sent her maid out to make some purchases.

"Ah!" she said a few minutes after, "my maid has forgotten to change my chemise."

"Allow me to take her place."

"Very well, but recollect that I give permission only to your eyes to take a share in the proceedings."

"Agreed!"

She unlaced herself, took off her stays and her chemise, and told me to be quick and put on the clean one, but I was not speedy enough, being too much engaged by all I could see.

"Give me my chemise," she exclaimed; "it is there on that small table."

"Where?"

"There, near the bed. Well, I will take it myself."

She leaned over towards the table, and exposed almost everything I was longing for, and, turning slowly round, she handed me the chemise which I could hardly hold, trembling all over with fearful excitement. She took pity on me, my hands shared the happiness of my eyes; I fell in her arms, our lips fastened together, and, in a voluptuous, ardent pressure, we enjoyed an amorous exhaustion not sufficient to allay our desires, but delightful enough to deceive them for the moment.

With greater control over herself than women have generally under similar circumstances, she took care to let me reach only the porch of the temple, without granting me yet a free entrance to the sanctuary.

A Note About the Author

Giacomo Casanova (1725–1798) was an Italian adventurer and author. Born in Venice, Casanova was the eldest of six siblings born to Gaetano Casanova and Zanetta Farussi, an actor and actress. Raised in a city noted for its cosmopolitanism, night life, and glamor, Casanova overcame a sickly childhood to excel in school, entering the University of Padua at the age of 12. After graduating in 1742 with a degree in law, he struggled to balance his work as a lawyer and low-level cleric with a growing gambling addiction. As scandals and a prison sentence threatened to derail his career in the church, Casanova managed to find work as a scribe for a powerful Cardinal in Rome, but was soon dismissed and entered military service for the Republic of Venice. Over the next several years, he left the service, succeeded as a professional gambler, and embarked on a Grand Tour of Europe. Towards the end of his life, Casanova worked on his exhaustive, scandalous memoirs, a 12-volume autobiography reflecting on a legendary life of romance and debauchery that brought him from the heights of aristocratic society to the lows of illness and imprisonment. Recognized for his self-styled sensationalism as much as he is for his detailed chronicling of 18th century European culture, Casanova is a man whose name is now synonymous with the kind of life he led—fast, fearless, and free.

A Note from the Publisher

Spanning many genres, from non-fiction essays to literature classics to children's books and lyric poetry, Mint Edition books showcase the master works of our time in a modern new package. The text is freshly typeset, is clean and easy to read, and features a new note about the author in each volume. Many books also include exclusive new introductory material. Every book boasts a striking new cover, which makes it as appropriate for collecting as it is for gift giving. Mint Edition books are only printed when a reader orders them, so natural resources are not wasted. We're proud that our books are never manufactured in excess and exist only in the exact quantity they need to be read and enjoyed.

bookfinity™

Discover more of your favorite classics with Bookfinity™.

- Track your reading with custom book lists.
- Get great book recommendations for your personalized Reader Type.
- Add reviews for your favorite books.
- AND MUCH MORE!

Visit **bookfinity.com** and take the fun Reader Type quiz to get started.

Enjoy our classic and modern companion pairings!

Classic & Modern

www.ingramcontent.com/pod-product-compliance
Lightning Source LLC
Chambersburg PA
CBHW021133020426
42331CB00005B/749